# FORGIVENESS IS YOUR SUPERPOWER

## STEPS TO EMOTIONAL HEALING & IMPROVED PERSONAL GROWTH

### S.L. MILLS

# CONTENTS

# DEDICATION

*This book is dedicated to my uncle,*

*-Robert Smith*

*We miss you!*

# INTRODUCTION

Forgiveness isn't a choice; it's an inevitable act woven into our daily lives. Forgiveness is the process that guides us through pain toward the path of healing and growth. I am sure you have heard that when you decide not to forgive someone, it's like drinking poison and expecting the other person to die. The only thing that happens is that you slowly poison your life with the resentment that builds up inside of you. However, your life doesn't have to be that way. Forgiveness can pave the way to a life free of anger and bitterness and free you from the chains of past experiences.

 *We must develop and maintain the capacity to forgive. He who is devoid of the power to forgive is devoid of the power to love.*

MARTIN LUTHER KING JR. IN A GIFT
OF LOVE

What is forgiveness? If you forgive someone, does that mean you are condoning their actions? Absolutely not! There are many misconceptions about forgiveness. One is that you are letting them off the hook for what they did when, in fact, you're letting yourself off the hook. When you resent someone else's actions, you chain yourself to them and the pain you experienced. You get stuck emotionally and can struggle to grow past it.

> *"Forgiveness is a process of feeling, understanding, and letting go that is a gift to oneself."*
>
> BANK LEES, 2018

When my uncle's murderers got off on a technicality after beating him to death, I was hurt, angry, and grieving. This brought me face-to-face with the reality of anger and resentment. Over time, I began to see that the anger wasn't helping me or changing the situation. When I finally understood the transformative power of forgiveness, I could release the anger and resentment that lived in my daily thoughts and consumed my life.

> *The weak can never forgive. Forgiveness is the attribute of the strong.*
>
> GANDHI

Everything in our lives consumes energy. Emotion is energy. When we constantly feel an overwhelming emotion, such as anger or resentment, and allow it to consume our thoughts, it takes considerable energy. Life is challenging at the best of times. If we have a family, work, or friends, these things take energy, too. We don't have an endless supply. If we constantly drain our resources with wasted emotion that isn't serving us, it can beat us down and stop us from growing and progressing in our lives.

My reason for writing this book is to share the transformative power of forgiveness and to illustrate how it helped me to move on from a painful situation and into growth and peace. I'm not claiming that forgiveness is easy. It might even be one of the most challenging tasks you've ever undertaken, but I promise you it's worth it.

It's important to understand that forgiveness takes time. It's part of a healing process and doesn't happen overnight. But if you're patient and walk through the steps with me, you will find yourself in a state of freedom, released from the chains of bitterness just as I was. Setbacks will happen. You might even wake up one morning feeling anger and hurt again, just as when it happened. This is normal, and you shouldn't be upset with yourself. One of the goals of this book is to set out the roadmap for you to follow, pointing out the pitfalls along the way so you don't have to undertake the journey alone. Many people, me included, have been on this journey, and I know you can do it too.

When you set out on a trip, you plan your route. You might use a map, but most people now use GPS on their phones or vehicles. Unless you plan on driving aimlessly, you will make sure you know the best route to get to where you're going. In the same way, if you want to reach a specific destination in your life, having a roadmap can take away the guesswork.

> *Forgive others not because they deserve forgiveness,*
> *but because you deserve peace.*

JOHNATHAN LOCKWOOD HALE

There are several steps to forgiveness, but the first is acknowledgment. You have to acknowledge the pain before you can even begin to deal with it. The steps to forgiveness are:

1. Acknowledgment
2. Understanding
3. Empathy
4. Decision
5. Release

Anger, resentment, guilt, and pain are only a few emotions you can expect to experience as you learn to let go and allow forgiveness to grow. It's okay to feel how you feel. We need to establish that first. No emotion is good or bad; they just are. It's vital to remind yourself of this during the process so you don't beat yourself up or feel that you're failing because you're angry. These emotions will come, and they will come in sometimes overwhelming waves. We are individual human beings, and we all have different needs and reactions to pain.

When I lost my uncle to a senseless crime, I wasn't sure I or my family would ever recover. I had to watch my father grieve over his brother and the rest of my family ask the question, "Why?" The truth is, there is rarely a cut-and-dried reason why something happens. In a crime, sometimes even the perpetrator doesn't know why. As humans, we want to know. We have the desire to make sense of things, and it can send us into a spiral of despair when we can't. This is what happened to my family.

When we sat in the courtroom and listened to the crime recounted, we had to experience the pain all over again. It's not something that any family should have to go through. At the end of it all, they got away without punishment. Now we had another "Why?" I could have gotten stuck here, and we were for some time, but I chose not to give those murderers another victim. That was my first step in the process of forgiveness.

I am in my 50s now. I have witnessed friends and family members who did not find forgiveness in their lives, and I can see how depressed, anxious, and unhappy these people are. They allowed their grief and anger to keep them trapped. I have written this book for everyone who has experienced pain and can't see their way to freedom.

I want this book to give you the steps that lead you to the reawakening of the possibilities of your life and the knowledge that forgiveness is indeed your superpower.

# CHAPTER 1
# ACKNOWLEDGEMENT

## THE FIRST STEP: ACKNOWLEDGING YOUR PAIN

**B**efore you can begin dealing with what has happened to you, you must first acknowledge that it happened. This may seem simplistic, but it's a vital part of the process and an essential first step. When you have a relationship conflict with someone, you need to validate each other's feelings before you can deal with the conflict. In the same way, you need to validate your own feelings before you can sort out how to deal with them.

The beginning of the process of forgiveness is empathy for yourself. Sometimes, the situation that happened to us makes us feel we should have stopped it or somehow been able to control it. Pain is not logical, so some of your feelings might not be logical, too, but that's okay. Your feelings exist for a reason, and you must be kind to yourself and validate them. You can never process your feelings fully if you refuse to validate them.

For example, if you make a mistake but refuse to acknowl-edge that you are at fault, you will never fix that flaw in yourself. To bring change, we must begin by acknowledging the incident. Feelings are no different. When you refuse to validate a feeling, it will continue to hold you hostage. If you want to release it, you must look it in the eye and say, "I see you." You don't have to do anything other than that because feelings are feelings. They aren't tangible; as I said, they might not even make sense to you. However, they are valid, and you have a right to feel how you feel. What you do about them is when things can take a different turn.

One of the most challenging things you can do is face pain. We are hard-wired to avoid anything that brings us pain, so the struggle to go against your very nature is tricky. I'm sure you've lived long enough to realize that the hard things in life bring us the most joy and peace. Think of a woman giving birth. It's one of the most brutal and painful things she'll ever do, and yet bringing a child into the world is so joyous. Let me tell you a story.

A friend of mine, let's call her Clara, was married, and her husband cheated on her. All the signs were there, but facing his betrayal was so frightening that she convinced herself he was the same man she believed she'd married over ten years ago. Even though he showed her in many ways that he wasn't the man she believed he was, she continued to live in the world she chose. Until she couldn't avoid it. He left and left her with nothing. She had no job or vehicle and had to move into her best friend's basement. Clara felt like her life was over.

Of course, Clara's husband blamed her for everything. For a time, she believed him until she began to see more clearly away from his constant talking. She realized he had been telling her all along what she should believe. With him no longer telling her, she began to see the truth. Then, her best friend told her about narcissism.

Clara began learning about her life and why she had ended up in a relationship with a man who would mistreat her. She realized it went back to her childhood. The pain that came flooding in was of the most brutal kind. She wanted nothing more than to escape. And yet she was stuck. She began to understand that there was a reason for her being in her situation. As she delved into the past, the pain became so overwhelming that all she wanted to do was run away from it.

Finally, she began to understand something. The more she tried to avoid the pain, the worse it got. She knew the relationship was something that her past pain had caused her to allow in her life, and she was determined never to be in this situation again. All of her reading and video-watching told her that the only way to stop the pain was to go through it. Clara wondered if she had the strength to face it.

She decided to try. This time, she faced it rather than run away or distract herself. She allowed herself to feel the pain. It hurt. A lot. And then it began to hurt less. The more she understood what had happened to her and how it affected her mind and emotions, the less it hurt. She felt stronger and less vulnerable. She saw her husband a few times as they began the divorce process, and she didn't miss him. She was glad he'd left. Before many months had passed, Clara hardly felt the pain at all. She began to feel whole. She realized that facing the pain and going through the healing process meant that she would never be hurt like that again.

Clara is now a strong, healthy woman living her best life. She healed and faced the pain, leaving the trap of her old way of thinking. Clara is glad she felt the pain, even though it was one of the hardest things she'd ever done, because that meant she could leave it behind.

## UNDERSTANDING THE IMPACT

Holding onto anger and resentment impacts all areas of your life. It doesn't matter if the situation is immense or minor; the anger and resentment affect your life. Please think about something that happened that made you angry. Think about what the person did to you and how you feel about it. Imagine yourself in that situation again, if you can, and why you feel justified in being angry and resentful. Now that you feel the feelings, take a step back from the situation and look at your whole life. Can you see where your feelings toward the situation and person(s) impact other areas of your life? Do you judge people based on what happened in the past? Maybe you don't trust men because you were betrayed by one. Maybe you struggle in your relationships with your children because you haven't forgiven your mother for what she did to you.

There are so many ways that resentment can cause problems in our lives. It can even be our general outlook on life. If you're angry and bitter, how can you be grateful? How can you enjoy the little things when your mind is filled with negative feelings? I'm sure you feel justified in your feelings. I'm not saying what happened to you was fair. When people hurt us, it's rarely fair. But you need to remember one thing. Hurt people, hurt people. I will say that over and over throughout this book because it's an important thing to remember. If you hang on to your pain, you will continue to hurt inside, and you will hurt others even if you don't mean to.

## *The Role of Grief*

Once you face your pain, you will begin to experience grief. Until you acknowledge and validate your feelings, you won't be able to go through the natural grieving process, which is a vital part of healing. In the introduction, we mentioned the five steps of forgiveness, which are similar to the grieving stages, and we will discuss them further now.

### 1. Acknowledgment

**A.** This is the first stage and the most essential. Without the acknowledgment and validation of what you've experienced, you can't begin the healing process. It's okay to be sad. It's okay to feel hurt and angry. As we discussed at the beginning of this chapter, feelings are just feelings. They can come and go, but what they won't do is be ignored. You might experience an escalation of feelings, especially anger, or your health may begin to break down.

**B.** Feelings have a way of being noticed. Begin the process by noticing and acknowledging the feelings from the painful situation and allow yourself to feel them. This is one of the most challenging parts of the process and why many people never allow themselves to begin healing. No one wants to feel pain, especially over one of the most hurtful things you've experienced. But once you allow yourself to feel it, it will begin to dissipate. It may take a while, but I can promise you it won't always hurt so much.

## 2. Understanding

**A.** When you seek an understanding of forgiveness and what happened to you, you take another step forward. You may never understand why the situation happened, but you can begin to understand its role in your life. Bad things happen to good people. Whether or not you believe in a higher power, seeing the why is usually challenging; sometimes, there isn't even a why. So rather than waste time asking, "Why me?" rather ask yourself, "Why not me?" and seek to understand how you can grow from the situation.

## 3. Empathy

**A.** I'm sure the last thing you want is to have empathy for the person(s) who caused you such grief. Many people's first reaction is to lash out or to get revenge. All that will do is cause you more pain, no matter what you think, while you're feeling the intense emotion of anger.

**B.** Once you begin to work on understanding, you may discover that the person who wounded you is also a hurt person. Hurt people, hurt people. When they don't seek empathy as you do, they will hurt others as they were hurt. Empathy is the way forward if you don't want to become that person. Realize that they have pain, colossal pain, that they have allowed to twist them into something you would never want to be.

## 4. Decision

**A.** Forgiveness is a decision. It's not something you fall into. You can fall into anger and bitterness, but you can't fall into forgiveness. You choose it for yourself and your life to release yourself from the chains that bind you to the situation that hurt you. You choose not to let it take over your life and destroy you. You choose to be and do better than the person who hurt you. You may feel they don't deserve forgiveness, but it's not about them. It's about you. And you deserve to be free.

## 5. Release

**A.** The final step is freedom. You walk away, your head held high, into a better, more peaceful life. Forgiveness takes hard work, but as you walk away from the pain, you will realize it has all been worth it.

## SELF-COMPASSION

You are just beginning this journey, so you can't expect yourself to get it right away. It will take time, and you must be patient with yourself, even if you think you aren't progressing quickly enough. That's okay. This is a personal journey, and you need to take it at a comfortable pace. If you try to push yourself or get upset and miss a step, you can delay or even roadblock your progress. The necessary thing is to let yourself feel how you feel but not to wallow in it. Feel it and move on. Feel compassion and love for your hurt self but be careful not to pamper the feeling. See it. Name it. And then release it. But be kind to yourself.

## BEYOND THE MYTHS: WHAT FORGIVENESS IS AND ISN'T

Forgiveness involves willfully putting aside resentment toward someone who has committed a wrong, been unfair or hurtful, or otherwise harmed you in some way. Forgiveness is not merely accepting what happened or ceasing to be angry. Instead, it involves a voluntary transformation of your feelings, attitudes, and behavior so that you are no longer dominated by resentment and can express compassion, generosity, or the like toward the person who wronged you (Forgiveness, n.d.).

Forgiveness isn't forgetting; it's a decision to release yourself from the situation that caused you pain. When you forgive, it's an internal process that usually doesn't involve the other person. Later, if they are open to it, you can address the situation with them and even tell them that you forgive them, but often, that isn't possible or even a good idea, depending on their state of mind. Sometimes, the person you need to forgive isn't even alive anymore. So, it's essential to understand that forgiveness is you deciding to let go of resentment and freeing yourself, but it doesn't mean you have to forget. And it definitely doesn't mean you should accept that what happened to you was okay.

### *Debunking Myths*

There are some myths out there that I want to address. It's important to understand that forgiveness isn't a weakness. It's quite the opposite. When you forgive the other person and release yourself from resentment and anger, you choose strength over weakness. I'm sure you realize by now that not only making the decision but going through the process of forgiveness isn't the easy road; it's the road less traveled. So, choosing to forgive is weak? Not at all! It's a much harder choice, but also the choice to put yourself first.

The other myth is that you need to reconcile or be in contact with the person you are forgiving. That isn't true. If it were, you wouldn't be able to forgive someone who has died or a murderer. Forgiveness, as we've already discussed, isn't about the other person; it's about acknowledging and dealing with your own pain, so reconciliation, while always a choice, doesn't have to be part of the equation. If the wrong perpetrated against you was committed by a family member and you desire to make things right with them, and they have apologized and desire to make things right with you, then that would be wonderful for all involved. Reconciliation is often the best-case scenario but sometimes isn't recommended.

If, for example, the person who wronged you isn't the least bit sorry and has no intention of making things right, you can leave them out of the scenario. You deal with your pain, release them from your life, and move on. Sometimes, the person is even dangerous or causes you continual pain. In that case, I would even recommend cutting them out of your life and choosing peace. That includes family members. Family members are those who love and treat you well, not those who abuse you. It's vital to make that distinction. Forgiveness isn't about allowing abuse in your life. It's about healing and moving away from abuse.

### The Power of Choice

The wonderful thing about forgiveness is that it's a choice you can make and not something forced upon you. When you go through a horrific experience, it can make you feel out of control. The thing that happened was something you couldn't stop. You couldn't go back and change the circumstances; it was all out of your control. That's often why we question and try to figure out if we could have avoided the situation if only, we had made a different choice. It's a search for a semblance of control.

You take control when you forgive and process your emotions around the incident. When you allow yourself to hang on to bitterness and anger, you are not in control; the situation and the person who wronged you are in control of you and your emotions. Choosing forgiveness is a beautiful way to take back your control, or another word for it, power. Now, you are choosing to let go of what happened, choosing not to let it rule your life, and choosing freedom.

When I chose to forgive my uncle's murderers, it was a powerful and emotional experience. I remember how the anger and bitterness flowed away from me, and I felt like I was taking control of my life. It was an experience I will never forget. The best feeling in the world is the freedom you feel after choosing the path of forgiveness.

## FORGIVENESS VS. RECONCILIATION: NAVIGATING THE DIFFERENCE

We mentioned reconciliation above and how it's not always necessary or recommended. Sometimes, it can be the best choice, but it's irrelevant for forgiveness. It's an entirely separate process. Forgiveness is how you deal with and release your pain, anger, and bitterness. Reconciliation isn't necessary for that to happen. Understanding the difference can help you realize you can forgive without speaking to or being near the person who wronged you.

Many people shy away from the forgiveness process because they misunderstand and think it requires reconciliation. This can cause them to stay in their pain and never find release. That's why it's vital to see that the two are entirely separate processes. If you choose to reconcile after you've gone through the process of forgiveness, this can bring you even more peace and resolution, but as I said, it isn't necessary.

You need to assess your situation and ask yourself, do I want, need, or even should I reconcile with the person who wronged me? First off, do they want to reconcile? You can't reconcile with someone all by yourself. This process requires both parties to participate fully, unlike the process of forgiveness. If they want reconciliation, you have to assess whether they are sincere and if you think they will continue the behavior that injured you in the first place. This comes under the topic of boundary setting, which we will discuss later in the chapter. Once you decide to go ahead with reconciliation, you can discuss the situation with the other party and hopefully come to a peaceful resolution. This isn't always possible, but it should be the end goal as it's the best possible outcome for peace in your life. Again, this is usually with family or for non-dangerous situations of criminal activity. Victims of crimes won't desire reconciliation with their abusers.

## THE ROLE OF EMPATHY IN FORGIVING OTHERS

Having empathy for the person who wronged you doesn't mean you agree with what they did. Empathy and compassion are necessary to the process of forgiveness. It might seem wrong to you or backward in some way, but it isn't. Many of us believe in some retribution, "karma," or something that makes things even. The trouble is, even if you believe in karma, you often never see it happen. It can be frustrating to realize the person may get away with their horrific behavior while innocent people suffer.

The world is unfair. It's an unfortunate truth; the sooner you accept it, the easier your life will be. You are only responsible for YOU. Your behavior is the only behavior you can control. Therefore, acting out of empathy and compassion toward those who wronged you has nothing to do with them and everything to do with you. It's not even about being "the bigger person," which can be condescending; it's about understanding that we all have pain, and some act out of pain rather than compassion.

Your choice to be forgiving, compassionate, and empathetic means that you will have a peaceful life and be able to move on from hurtful situations quickly. The person who is acting out their pain will continue to live in that pain for all of their life unless they make the same choice. That alone should make you feel empathy for them. They may have experienced things you could not even imagine or have never gone through. It's a truth that no one truly understands another person's pain. Remember, it's not an excuse for their behavior, but you're not responsible for them. You are only responsible for your response to their behavior.

"When you accept your blunders, you practice compassion. You understand that if you make mistakes, others make them, too. Nobody's perfect" (Zugaro, 2022).

Part of you may ask, "Why me? Why is it up to me to do the right thing even when they did something horrible to me?" It's because you want to live a better, healthier, and more peaceful life. Bitterness can affect your health. There have been studies done to suggest that anger can be a precursor to cancer. "There is evidence to show that suppressed anger can be a precursor to the development of cancer, and also a factor in its progression after diagnosis" (Thomas et al., 2000). So, I ask you again, why not you? Having a healthy, positive life means you do the hard work. If it were easy, we'd all be living in a Utopia.

## SELF-FORGIVENESS: THE JOURNEY BEGINS WITHIN

I'm sure you've heard that to truly love others, you must love yourself. This is also true of forgiveness. Sometimes, when we refuse to forgive others, it's because we haven't forgiven ourselves, either for what we perceive is our fault in the situation or for something much earlier. Someone said it so perfectly that I have to quote them.

"When someone hurts you, you get angry with yourself. 'How could I be so stupid? Why did I trust them? I should've seen the signs earlier!' You project your anger toward yourself on others, which makes forgiveness and healing impossible. This traps you in a toxic spiral, unable to let go—unable to stop hurting yourself" (Zugaro, 2022).

I couldn't have put it better. Indeed, we often get angry at ourselves for not seeing the danger in the situation. This is especially true of those who are crime victims. They might say things like:

- Why did I walk home? I should have taken a cab.
- Why did I stay at the party when my friends left?
- I should have seen how he treated his mother, other girlfriends, co-workers, etc., and known who he was.
- I shouldn't have...
- I should have...

The fact is, we don't always know, nor should we expect ourselves to. To live life well, we must take a certain number of risks. That's as it should be, and sometimes those risks mean you get into a bad situation through no fault of your own. You must forgive yourself first if you're going to be able to move on from the situation.

## THE RIPPLE EFFECT OF FORGIVENESS ON YOUR HEALTH

Our feelings affect our health. There's no way around that. We aren't just bodies or minds; we are both together. What affects our minds affects our bodies and vice versa. When we carry anger in our bodies, we are in continual flight or fight mode. We never wholly relax, taxing our immune system and adrenal glands. Forgiveness hugely impacts your health by lowering the risk of heart attacks, improving your choles-terol levels, getting deeper and more restful sleep, and lowering blood pressure, anxiety, and stress. So, if forgive-ness causes all this to happen, imagine what holding bitter-ness and anger is doing to your body, not to mention your mind (Forgiveness: Your Health..., 2021).

We store unexpressed emotions in our bodies. "It is well-established that emotions affect the body as well as the mind. If a person has persistent or unresolved feelings that cause physical symptoms, they may feel as though these emotions are trapped or stuck" (Murnan, 2023). You can have feelings like butterflies in the stomach when you're nervous or anxious, jaw tension, or pain in the chest, which feels like heartbreak. These are all emotions manifesting in the phys-ical body despite having no physical cause.

I heard a story some time ago about a man convinced he was going to die of a heart attack. He kept showing up at the hospital complaining of pain in his chest, but the doctors could find no cause or symptoms beyond the pain he was experiencing. They would do a full workup and then send him home. He soon returned with the same complaint. This happened about 4 or 5 times until one day, he turned up with an actual heart attack and died. The reason for his death wasn't negligence. The doctors didn't miss anything. He believed that he was going to die from a heart attack because his father was at the same age, which caused his actual attack. His fear and beliefs were intense enough to manifest in his physical body.

## SETTING BOUNDARIES: FORGIVENESS DOES NOT MEAN TOLERANCE

Before we move on from this topic, there is another vital topic: setting boundaries. When you have someone in your life who consistently causes you harm or grief, consider removing them from your life. You should consider setting boundaries if you aren't willing to do that. First, what is a boundary?

* * *

Amaya was a fun-loving person who had many friends in her life. Her apartment had an open-door policy, so her friends would come and go regularly. Most of their friends would text her before showing up, but she never really minded when they would knock on her door without a text. There was one friend, however, who would show up at inappropriate times and nearly every day. All of Amaya's friends knew she was a night owl, so her friends usually stayed away until at least noon. One friend, Carrie, however, would regularly knock on Amaya's door as early as 8 am. Carrie wouldn't text. She would just show up. Amaya asked her often not to come over so early, but Carrie would ignore Amaya's request and show up even earlier the next day.

Amaya began ignoring the door, but Carrie wouldn't knock just a few times. If Amaya didn't answer, knocking would turn to pounding, and then Amaya's neighbors would complain to her later. It made Amaya angry, especially when Carrie would ignore her requests and laugh about it later with their friends, calling Amaya grumpy and "pissy pants."

Amaya considered telling Carrie she was no longer welcome to come over, but she knew it would cause problems in their friend's group because they had all been friends since they were children. Outside of this one issue, she liked Carrie, so she realized it was time to be more direct.

Amaya asked Carrie to come over one morning at 10 am. Carrie, as usual, showed up earlier, at nine. Amaya had done this on purpose to make a point. She sat Carrie down and discussed the issue. Amaya said it wasn't about Carrie bothering her. The thing that made Amaya so upset was that she had no respect for Amaya's request. Amaya had set a boundary, and Carrie had disregarded it. Amaya told her friend that she was explicitly setting a boundary of noon when she was unavailable and that if Carrie respected her, she would honor her request. At first, Carrie was upset. Amaya realized that Carrie had issues with boundaries because of her upbringing. Amaya explained to her that people need boundaries not to build up resentment toward the people in their lives. After much discussion, Carrie agreed to the boundary. They went on to have a better relationship, and Amaya no longer had to be angry and frustrated with her friend.

\* \* \*

Boundaries are vital to human relationships, not just in forgiveness. You need to decide if what happened to you was because someone didn't respect your boundaries or because they weren't strong enough. Sometimes, people hurt us because we haven't set boundaries.

To protect ourselves, we must be clear about what behavior we will accept and what we won't. When we clarify this to the people in our lives, we also give them an idea of what they should expect from us. If they struggle with boundaries, as Carrie did, we can help them understand their importance and maybe even assist them in setting boundaries in their own lives.

If you struggle with setting boundaries, this might help. Boundaries aren't about controlling others but are there to protect you, your time, and your space. Imagine if Amaya had allowed her friend to continue her behavior. She would have struggled to function in her life with a lack of sleep. She would be constantly frustrated, maybe even irritated. Despite her best intentions, the relationship would eventually crack, affecting their entire friend group. Also, Amaya would probably one day explode at her friend, who would be taken by surprise because Amaya had never been honest about her feelings.

Boundaries protect relationships and make them more palatable and safer for everyone involved. So, if you are struggling to keep to your boundaries, remember that you're doing it for yourself, the other person, and the relationship.

You might be saying that's all great, but how exactly do you set boundaries and know they are proper? Boundaries are personal. It's a bit like personal space. If you feel uncomfortable when someone steps too close to you, they have invaded your personal space. For some people, their personal space boundary might be mere inches, but for others, it might be a foot or more. You will know when someone has crossed a boundary when you feel uncomfortable.

The way to set them is to decide what behavior is acceptable to you and what isn't. Don't be afraid to make the decision. It's a human right to decide who and what to accept into your life. Once you have established that, you won't need to tell anyone. The way you treat others will make your boundaries clear to most people. Only when a person repeatedly encroaches on your boundary will you have to inform them of your stance. Once or twice is okay, but beyond that, it's time to be honest and have a heart-to-heart. If they reject your boundary setting, you must choose your next step. Limit your interaction with them, or possibly remove them from your life. But whatever you choose, you have the right to protect your peace.

## FORGIVENESS AS A LIFESTYLE: CULTIVATING A FORGIVING MINDSET

It might seem like a lot of effort to practice forgiveness, but like anything, the more you practice, the better you get. Forgiveness isn't so much an action as a way of being. It's a mindset. When you operate from a place of forgiveness, it will be difficult to offend you. When you see behavior, you don't accept, you either address it or walk away. You are the one in control of your life and what you allow. As Dr. Phil said, "You teach people how to treat you" (McGraw, 2014).

When you meet someone new, your reactions to their behavior tell them what you will and will not accept. This is how you teach people who you are and what you believe. You don't usually have to sit down and explain it to others. A lot of human communication is nonverbal and intuitive. There will be people with whom you will need to go further, but most of them will understand quickly enough. As you continue confidently, it will get much more manageable.

It is an illusion that we have control over our lives. Things happen, often daily, that are entirely out of our control. The only things we have actual control over are our reactions and behavior. Embracing vulnerability can be a strength. That may seem counterintuitive, but it's not. Being vulnerable doesn't mean you allow the people around you to treat you how they desire; it means you keep your walls down and are open to whatever life brings your way. When you know your boundaries, you know how you need to react to things to keep yourself as safe as it's possible to be in life. You can be open to new experiences and have a wonderful time, but you know how to walk away when something makes you uncomfortable.

Many people choose to be victims. It's a way of taking the responsibility away from themselves. They think if they are victims, they aren't responsible for the results of their life. It's like thinking, "Someone else did this to me. They hurt me, so I'm going to hide away in my house so no one else can hurt me." Can you see how that only hurts the "victim" further? I don't believe in victim mentality. It's self-limiting and guarantees further pain. Stepping outside the victim mentality and choosing to be an overcomer is empowering and brings life-long peace.

There are many ways to foster a forgiving mindset, which I will discuss further in later chapters. One fantastic way is to keep a gratitude journal. Humans are so adaptable that we can quickly forget the positive things we experience. A gratitude journal helps to keep these things in our minds and fosters a sense of outward sight that helps us see when good things are in front of us so we don't miss out.

In the next chapter, we will discuss the obstacles to adopt a forgiveness mindset and how you can effectively dismantle them and free yourself forever!

# CHAPTER 2
# UNDERSTANDING BARRIERS TO FORGIVENESS

## UNPACKING EMOTIONAL BAGGAGE: IDENTIFYING WHAT HOLDS YOU BACK

When you're struggling to deal with emotions from a past issue, you might need to check in with yourself to ask if you have other emotional baggage that might be holding you back.

First, let's discuss what emotional baggage means and how it might hold you back from experiencing the best of your life.

According to Sabrina Romanoff, PsyD, a clinical psychologist and professor at Yeshiva University, the term "emotional baggage" refers to unfinished emotional issues, stressors, pain, and difficulties we've experienced that continue to take up space in our minds and affect our present relationships" (Gupta, 2023).

When you go through an experience similar to something that wounded you in the past, it might trigger an overreaction or an emotional response that doesn't seem to fit the situation. This can be due to past emotional trauma or emotional baggage that you are still carrying around. This is why forgiveness is so important. If you don't go through the process of forgiving and letting go of the trauma, you will continue to carry it around and pile new emotional baggage on top until all of it weighs you down and makes it difficult to function.

One of the first steps in figuring out if you have emotional baggage is to think about past trauma and unresolved conflicts. It may go as far back as your childhood or be something more recent, but if when you think about that situation, strong emotions or reactions arise, you may have some issues that need resolving.

There are a few signs of emotional trauma that may help you to identify what is holding you back from success in your life.

## DIFFICULTY WITH TRUSTING OTHERS

Trust is a big one. Once burned, twice shy is a cliche because it's how humans learn. If you touch a hot stove and get burned, you learn never to do that again. If someone "burns" you, you learn to be less trusting.

If you struggle with trust, there is probably a good reason for it. We often shame ourselves for struggling with something when there is usually a good reason for it. Shaming yourself doesn't help the situation or help you to get past it. So, I would suggest you let yourself off the hook and allow yourself to dive into what caused you to lose the ability to trust. The answer probably lies with your previous trauma.

It's not comfortable to face trauma but looking it in the eye is the only way to deal with it. Acknowledge what happened and then accept that it happened. Only then will you be able to move on and heal.

## 1. Fear

A. If you find yourself fearful in either a specific situation or in general, a trauma probably caused it. For example, if someone is afraid of being a passenger in a car, they might have experienced a car crash where they or someone they love was injured.

B. Children tend to be born trusting and have little fear. It's trauma that causes these things in our lives as we grow. A child falls off their bike and then begins to fear riding. Another child hurts them, and they learn to be cautious around other children.

## 2. Anger

A. An overabundance of anger, or even a "bad temper," can indicate buried trauma. I have a good friend who is generally a happy person, but the smallest thing can cause him to fly into a sudden rage that is out of proportion to the situation. Frustration quickly turns into anger, which escalates into rage.

B. Often, anger is directed at others, but the source is usually anger at ourselves. We might feel anger because we were helpless in the trauma or because we are frustrated that we can't get past it. The only way to solve the quick temper problem is to deal with the source.

## 3. Guilt

**A.** This is a big one. Many people feel guilty and have no idea why. Some believe there can even be a generational trauma component. For our purposes, though, we will focus on the trauma that has happened to you in this lifetime. You might feel guilt even if you weren't the one that caused the trauma. Women who are victims of rape are one example of this. Even though they are victims, they often feel they did something to bring on the attack, when that is never the case.

**B.** When you feel guilty, but you're not sure why, it could be indicative of some trauma that you need to deal with.

One point I want to make here is that these emotions are merely symptoms of the issue. Anger, fear, frustration, and many other emotions are just symptoms of a root cause that goes down deep. The only way to effectively deal with the symptoms is to deal with the root. It's like pulling a weed. If you don't get the root, the weeds will return.

There are many causes of unresolved traumas. There could have been childhood abuse. Even if you think it didn't happen to you but can't find any other reason for your emotions, you may have blocked it out of your memories. Our minds are powerful, and their job is to protect us. Even by giving us fear or anxiety, it's the mind's way of keeping us out of harm's way. Blocking out painful memories is another way. If you suspect you have blocked out trauma, going to someone who specializes in helping with blocked memories is vital, as you don't want to mess around with something you don't understand. Minds are powerful, but messing around with them can cause irrevocable damage if a professional does not supervise the treatment.

## STRATEGIES FOR ADDRESSING TRAUMA

One of the best ways to examine your life and try to understand yourself is by journaling. We will discuss it in more detail later, but having a daily journal practice has helped so many people. We all have different ways to express ourselves, but language is universal. Some struggle with verbal expression, so writing is often the best way for them to speak.

Journaling is like sitting down with yourself and having a conversation. I practice it daily, and I'm often surprised by what I write. Through writing in my journal, I have figured out many things.

If you don't find writing easy and prefer to talk, then talk therapy might be your best course of action. There are so many different types of professionals that it shouldn't be too difficult to find someone that you can relate to and who can help you sort out the trauma you've experienced.

Another way to examine your inner life is meditation. This might be something to try if you struggle with writing and are not interested in talk therapy. Sometimes, your mind gets more active when you get quiet and still. This is often the most significant struggle people have with meditation. They think that you must quiet your mind and have no thoughts. That's not the case. Maybe someone practicing for hours a day for many years might get to that place, but I don't believe that's the point of meditation. For me, I sit quietly and let my thoughts flow. I don't try to stop them, but I don't follow them. When I practice non-resistance, my thoughts are calm. The ones that don't matter often fall away, and then I'm left with my subconscious telling me what I need to know. That, for me, is what meditation is all about—communing with my inner self and unbiased listening.

## THE FEAR OF WEAKNESS

One of the greatest barriers to forgiveness is the fear of being seen as weak. Some people think that if they forgive someone who did them wrong, they'll be perceived as weak or religious (turning the other cheek) and will be preyed upon by someone else. Or it's the ego and not wanting to be the one to give in.

All of these are misconceptions. If you think forgiving is easy and holding a grudge is difficult, you have it backward. Deciding to forgive is one of the most challenging things to do. That's why it's essential to understand why you need to do it. If you don't realize that forgiving is the path to freedom, it will be easier to hold on to the pain and anger.

When your ego stands in the way, that's a problem. Mankind has had this issue since we first began. Think of stories like Romeo and Juliet and Cain and Abel, and I'm sure you can fill in the blank with someone you know or even yourself.

Our egos can both help and hinder us. The ego should give us a healthy sense of self-worth, but when it gets in the way of progress in our lives, it needs to be set aside.

When I was young, I read an inspiring story of forgiveness that has never left me. It's about a young woman, Corrie Ten Boom, a Dutch watchmaker who believed that all people, regardless of race, were precious. Corrie, along with her sister, Betsie, took in Jewish refugees and hid them from the Germans. In her book, The Hiding Place, she writes about how she and her family were discovered and arrested. They were arrested and placed in a concentration camp.

Corrie's sister, Betsie, died just twelve days before Corrie was released. It turned out to be a clerical error, and the others she'd been imprisoned with were sent to the gas chamber. Despite losing her sister and several other members of her family and enduring hardship and pain, soon after the war, Corrie went back to Germany and forgave those who harmed her, her family, and millions of Jews. Corrie understood there was no excuse for the evil people's actions, but that's not why she forgave. She did it because she understood what this book is all about. For her to become truly free, she needed to release herself from the anger and hatred she had every right to feel for what happened to her. As a result of choosing the path of forgiveness, she was no longer imprisoned but lived a life free of anger and resentment and inspired many to do the same.

If Corrie had chosen her anger over forgiveness, she would have essentially locked herself back up in that prison and kept herself there for the rest of her life. Choosing forgiveness is the same as unlocking that door and stepping out of jail and into freedom.

## ANGER, BITTERNESS, AND THEIR GRIP ON YOU

When someone wrongs you, it's perfectly natural to feel angry. You should feel the anger. Don't judge your feelings; allow them to be present. Sit with them. Allow them to wash over you. Then, allow them to wash away. Feelings are temporary. They only become permanent when you hold onto them and replay the events that brought them into being.

It's tempting to replay the event and continue to feel those emotions because it justifies your anger. If you remind yourself of what happened, you can feel that you are right to feel angry. I'm not disagreeing, but you can quickly trap yourself in a rage cycle. You replay the event and feel the anger; the justification causes it to flare hotter, and on it goes. How does this help you?

When you choose to release the anger and bitterness it doesn't mean you forget the situation. You allow the sting of it to fade and keep only the lesson. What do I mean by that? Life is about lessons. Remember what I said about the lesson of the hot stove? Lessons are meant for us to learn from them and then move on to new lessons. If we take the lesson of the hot stove and apply it to the anger situation, it will look like this: You burn your hand on the stove and get angry about it. Every day, you pick at the scab and make it bleed, and you get angry again. The next day, you do the same, and on and on, every day, making the scab bleed. You never let the wound heal, and you continue to hurt yourself repeatedly. If you allowed the wound to heal, you only had to experience the pain once. The memory would remain, reminding you never to touch the stove again. Do you see how silly and self-defeating it is to pick open a half-healed wound? It's no different when you continue to enrage yourself and feel bitterness when you remind yourself again and again how you were wounded.

## HOW TO RELEASE ANGER

### 1. Self-Awareness

A. Being aware of your emotions helps you recognize when you are spiraling into anger. It doesn't help you to allow your emotions to control you and not pay attention to them. Instead, ask yourself what is really going on inside. Emotions aren't just random, even though they might feel like it. They come from something, and being self-aware helps you track the source and deal with the anger in order to release it.

B. Sitting quietly and paying attention to your thoughts is a great way to notice what's happening in your mind and heart. Without paying attention, we can often go about our lives mindlessly and live in a reactive rather than proactive state. This means we can live for years without truly understanding what has caused the anger that seems to come from nowhere.

## 2. Mindfulness and Deep Breathing

**A.** Once you become aware of your anger and bitterness and understand what has caused it, you may struggle with the next step: not allowing it to control your life any longer. Sitting with the anger, rather than acting it out, is a healthy way of acknowledging it without allowing it to harm you or others.

**B.** Deep breathing during the overwhelming emotion can help to calm your nervous system and allow the anger to dissipate.

## 3. Journaling

**A.** Journaling is one of the best ways to connect with your subconscious and understand your emotions.

**B.** There's a reason many therapists use journaling as a tool for helping their patients heal. We often don't understand what's happening inside our minds until we write it down.

**C.** Daily journaling might seem like a colossal commitment, but it pays off in huge dividends, especially when you are actively working on healing. You'll have ups and downs, but as you journal daily, you'll begin to see your progress. Looking back months or years later, you'll be shocked at how far you've come.

## 4. Communication

**A.** Having someone to talk to, like a trusted friend, can help you sort out your emotions and let go of the anger.

**B.** Going to a therapist and engaging in talk therapy can also help. Having someone who understands the situation and how it can affect someone can give you some good advice on dealing with it. At the very least, talking is the best therapy.

**C.** Use "I" statements to avoid blame when describing how you feel, especially when communicating with family and friends.

## 5. Exercise

**A.** There's something very soothing about physical exercise. Depending on your physical fitness, going for a walk or a run can help soothe your anger.

**B.** Playing a sport, like tennis or squash, is an excellent outlet for anger because you're taking it out on a ball rather than a person.

**C.** Installing a punching bag in your basement or garage can also be a great way to release the anger that builds up for you to process it.

## 6. Creative Expression

**A.** Engaging in a hobby or any creative activity is also a great way to release the anger and frustration that may be building up. Creativity is soothing and allows you to express yourself in a way you might not normally do.

**B.** As they say, music soothes the savage beast. Playing the piano, drums, or another instrument is a wonderful way to soothe yourself and express your creativity. Even if you don't play an instrument, you can take lessons. Think about what instrument you have always been interested in.

**C.** Knitting, or any other yarn craft, has long been known to be soothing and a wonderful outlet for creativity and stress release.

## 7. Gratitude

**A.** This is the perfect opportunity to focus on everything you're grateful for. When you are angry over something, it can overshadow all the good things you have going on. Gratitude is a way of reminding yourself that not everything is bleak.

**B.** A gratitude journal can keep the good things at the forefront of your mind.

**C.** Making a habit of saying thank you to the people around you and to yourself daily is a good way of reminding yourself and others that you are grateful for them and what they contribute to your life.

## 8. Boundaries

**A.** Sometimes, the people who refuse to abide by our boundaries can trigger us and cause anger to flare. Usually, a crossed boundary caused the situation in the first place, so when someone does the same thing to us, it's triggering.

**B.** Having firm boundaries is vital to maintaining peace of mind and helping regulate your emotions.

## 9. Seek Professional Help

**A.** If your anger is out of control, you should contact a professional. It doesn't mean you're weak. Needing help and not asking for it is much weaker than reaching out. It shows you're willing to do what it takes to live your best life.

**B.** There are many professionals out there, so seek out someone who understands your situation and the struggle you're having. You can interview different therapists until you find someone with whom you feel comfortable opening up.

**C.** Anger management classes can also give you the tools to manage your emotions.

## 10. Reflect and Adjust

**A.** Regular reflection helps you assess your progress. If you've been journaling, reading over your past entries once a month is a great way to see how things are going.

**B.** Depending on your chosen method above, you can continue to repeat it as often as possible to see if it's helping you. If not, try a different method or several until you discover the best way to help yourself.

**C.** Scheduling time for yourself can be a great way to reflect. Take a walk by yourself, sit and listen to music, and give yourself some reflection time. Ask yourself, "How am I doing?"

Releasing anger and bitterness involves self-awareness, healthy outlets, communication, and self-care. Consistent effort and a combination of some of these practical steps can contribute to a more positive and emotionally balanced life.

## OVERCOMING VICTIM MENTALITY

What does it mean to have a victim mentality? You might say, "Something horrible happened to me, and therefore, I'm a victim." In the dictionary sense, yes, you're a victim. Someone committed a crime against you or caused you great harm and grief, that makes you a victim. Being a victim is static. It happened, and now that it's no longer happening, you're no longer a victim. Now you WERE a victim. Do you see the difference? If you continue to play over the scenario and continue to feel the horrible feelings you felt, you are now making yourself a victim, not the person who made you one in the first place.

It's about your mindset, not about what happened to you. It's what you do with it that matters. Many people are victims, but many live happy, successful lives after. When you continue to blame the other person for your pain, you allow yourself to keep on feeling it. Of course, they caused the pain, but when you refuse to release the pain, you are now causing the pain you feel. The point is, you're in charge. It may not feel like it but let me explain further.

When you refuse to be a victim, you become a survivor. You survived. That's the point. So now you're no longer a victim but a survivor, and a survivor survives and thrives. Holding a grudge (resentment) is a way of holding on to the feelings you feel. It's a survival mechanism; your biology helps to remind you of what that person did so you'll protect yourself in the future. We don't need these kinds of mechanisms in our modern world. They only hold us back from experiencing freedom. It doesn't mean you shouldn't be cautious in the future; just don't tie yourself to that situation.

> *If you have low self-esteem, poor coping skills, are embarrassed by the hurt, and/or have a short temper you may be even more likely to hold a grudge.*
>
> VANBUSKIRK, 2023.

When your ego is involved, letting go of resentment can be more challenging. You were embarrassed, and you can't get past that feeling. People with low self-esteem often react like victims because it gives them a sense of self-righteousness and makes them feel important. We all get hurt sometimes and have many reasons to hold resentment, but it never serves us.

A person with a victim mentality feels that they are never at fault for what happens in their life. They often feel that the world is out to get them, and they have no control over anything. This often starts with an actual situation where they were a victim, but it escalates into everything that happens around them because they never dealt with the first situation. This is why it's vital to process and deal with the emotions and the situation, or you risk never getting past the stage of grief.

When you accept that you're human and make mistakes just like everyone else in the world, you should be able to take responsibility for your mistakes. Often, it's difficult for someone to admit they are wrong because of low self-esteem or because they were never taught to take responsibility for things by their parents. This is a common thing in the current generation of children. When you don't accept responsibility for what you do in your life, you can't learn from it and release yourself from the results of your actions by apologizing and forgiving yourself.

## FORGIVING WITHOUT AN APOLOGY?

One of the most significant barriers to forgiveness is the fear of facing the other person or knowing that the other person isn't sorry. This is very common and not the barrier you might think. It doesn't matter if the person is ready to apologize, if they're sorry, or if they even think they did nothing wrong because forgiveness isn't about them. It's an internal process that only depends on your willingness to release yourself from the chains of bitterness and hatred.

It may be challenging to let go of the situation when you feel you deserve an apology. That person did something horrible to you, and you may feel that they should acknowledge it at the very least! I can attest that this is one of the hardest things to overcome. We want justice but often don't get it, just like my uncle. My family was horrified to learn that my uncle's murderers weren't going to be punished for the horrific crime they had committed. Where is the justice in that? Too often, our justice system seems to be anything but just.

I don't have to tell you that life isn't fair. If you've lived for any time at all, you already know this. That doesn't mean you have to be a victim. Fair isn't keeping your anger and bitterness. Would it have mattered to those men if I held on to my anger? Not for a second. They are criminals and probably don't even have remorse. So, if I lived the rest of my life expecting an apology or acknowledgment of their wrongdoing, I would die with the same anger without ever getting the apology.

I know we keep saying the same things, like forgiveness is about you, but that's because it's a foreign concept. Anger and bitterness are easy, but forgiveness is not. I wouldn't need to write this book or share my story if it were. I want to see others have the same freedom I've discovered.

We've already discussed empathy, self-reflection, and acceptance. These are paths to freedom and joy.

## LETTING GO OF CONTROL

You have no control. I'm going to repeat that. You have NO CONTROL. It's hard to swallow, but the sooner you choke it down, the better. We may be able to control a few things in life, such as the actions we take or don't, but we have no control over the things that happen to us, or the actions others take.

Once you understand and accept this fact, you will understand your role in life and how to handle what others do. It isn't easy, but it makes life easier. Parents know that they can teach their children how to conduct themselves, but ultimately, the kids will do what they choose, especially after they're grown up and out of their parent's home. We only have control over our own actions and attitudes.

Think about a time when you tried to go on a diet or decided to change a bad habit. How did it go? Unless you're an incredibly disciplined person, you probably struggled. We all do. So, if it's that hard to control yourself, imagine trying to control another person. No one wants to be controlled, and it's not a nice thing to do.

Releasing yourself from the desire to control can change your life. Acceptance of the things you cannot change is one of the creeds of Alcoholics Anonymous. When you focus on the one thing you can change, your behavior, life gets a lot simpler.

When you choose to accept the lack of control, you feel free. I can't even describe the feeling that came over me when I made this choice. It was like I'd been carrying this heavy pack filled with boulders. I set it down one day and never picked it up again. Not having to carry that around with me everywhere I go is a relief of significant proportions!

## THE CHALLENGE OF FORGIVING OURSELVES

Usually, the hardest person to forgive is yourself. To express true love, you need to be able to love yourself first, and the same is true of forgiveness. We often experience excessive guilt far beyond the situation that might be misplaced. Guilt is a tricky emotion. It can attach itself to you even when you have no reason to feel it. Often, guilt comes from a different source or experience and will color everything in our lives. I have met people who seem to feel guilty about everything. Usually, that person had a childhood filled with criticism or even abuse. Letting go of guilt is vital because it doesn't serve you; it will only hold you back. If you have something to make right, make it right, but don't hang on to guilt.

We talked about empathizing with the person(s) who wronged you. What about having empathy for yourself? That is just as important. You are taking a huge step by reading this book, and you should be proud of yourself for trying to change your life. You're the only one holding yourself back, so making that decision and going through the process will be the best gift you have ever given yourself.

You can try writing a letter of forgiveness to yourself using words like "I forgive myself for..." Writing it down, making it tangible, and even burning it once you're done is a symbolic way of release. Fire is cleansing. I've done it myself. Sometimes, I even write a letter to someone who hurt me and never send it. The point was in writing it down. That was when the release came, and I didn't need to take it further.

In our modern society, we don't generally practice many rituals for mental health. Rituals used to be a huge part of the human experience for good reason. They can help mark a specific turning point in our lives, and having a ritual to look back on can help make it feel like you're taking a step in a new direction.

A friend of mine had a boyfriend she knew wasn't good for her. She had to break up with him but loved him and was having trouble letting him go. She finally talked with him and broke it off, but she would see him occasionally and feel all the feelings again. She decided her heart needed a ritual to make it final. During a trip to the lake, she brought home a pretty stone to remember the day. She'd hung on to the stone, and she knew it was a good representation of the relationship.

My friend took the stone to a river and said goodbye to her boyfriend. She said she would always love him, but it was time to let him go. With those words, she threw the stone into the river and imagined the relationship flowing away with the current. She said after this ritual, she could release him and begin to heal.

* * *

A ritual that has meaning for you can be a fantastic way of putting a pin in your situation and saying here is where it ends. With the ritual, you can find release and move on.

In the next chapter, we'll dive deeper into practical steps toward the freedom of forgiveness.

# CHAPTER 3
# PRACTICAL STEPS TOWARD FORGIVENESS

## JOURNALING FOR FORGIVENESS

One thing common to most people when dealing with pain is chaotic emotions. It can be challenging to sort through your feelings and to know how to deal with them. The other aspect is the need for a safe space to express those emotions, which can often feel ugly and shameful. Those feelings can be scary to express to someone else when they're even hard to admit to ourselves. We can tell ourselves not to judge our emotions, but it can be challenging to put into practice.

A journal can be a safe place of expression. If you're afraid of someone reading your journal, you can find a good hiding place or buy one with a lock. Hopefully, the people you share a home with respect your right to privacy, but if you don't feel safe, you can take the necessary steps to safeguard your journal. It should feel like a trusted friend to whom you can express all your emotions and who you know won't judge you.

You may think of the time you'll spend journalling as extra time you don't have, but I suggest you think of it as something that will pay back in so many dividends that it would be a waste of time not to journal. One way to make it more desirable to sit down and journal is to make it special. I like to buy pretty journals. They have a padded cover with pretty designs and beautiful smooth-lined paper inside. Writing in them is a pleasure. I also bought myself a special gel pen that I only use for my journal. This way, I make it a treat to sit down and write. It makes me feel pampered and helps me to open my journal daily.

Writing your thoughts down may be difficult at first. There is no right or wrong way to do it. Sometimes, writing whatever comes to you can be like a thought dump. I often must write down my immediate thoughts about what happened that day or the day before. They aren't necessary, but getting into deeper themes is much easier once they are cleared out. It's like wiping away the surface debris before I can start digging deeper.

If you commit to journaling daily, you will find it easier as time goes on. Many years ago, I committed to "Morning Pages" after reading *The Artist's Way*, a book by Julia Cameron. If you haven't read her book, I would suggest it as a great one to learn how to journal effectively. She developed the method to clear the mind for creative writing, but I've found the method to help with journaling in general and to clear the consciousness of debris to make way for deeper reflection.

Julia describes morning pages as stream-of-consciousness writing. She suggests you write three pages about anything going on in your life.

**Example**

- I need to change the kitty litter today...
- John told me about his friend from work who is a mechanic and might be able to fix our car...
- My sister is coming next week, and I need to plan what we will do for her visit...

These are just mundane things, but they are immediate. They are what's on your mind at the moment. Once you clear them out of the way, you will find other thoughts flowing in, maybe even things you haven't thought of before. I usually write less than one page of mundane thoughts before the real stuff starts coming out, but then I've been journaling for over 20 years. Now, I usually don't even write mundane thoughts. That will also happen for you in time, but I've gotten a lot of practice as a writer. That's the beauty of journaling. It will be different for everyone, so make it work for YOU!

Once you've journaled for a while, you'll see patterns in your thoughts and feelings. You'll see where an event or something someone said causes you to react a certain way. You'll maybe even see how different days or different times in the month affect you based on what's happening in your life. A journal gives you both a big-picture view and a microscopic view of your life and feelings at the same time. I have many journals now, and I can look back on my life and see the changes and how I healed. It's so powerful!

When you begin journaling, you might go blank and have no idea what to write. That's okay! It's normal. If you need a prompt or two, try the ones below.

**To Begin:**

- What happened yesterday that caused me joy?
- Who is someone in my life for whom I am grateful? Why am I grateful for them?
- What is a dream vacation I would take if I had the money?
- What does my perfect "me" day look like?

**On Forgiveness:**

- What does forgiveness mean to me?
- Am I afraid to let go of the pain? Why do I think that is?
- What did the situation or person(s) cause me to feel? Don't be afraid to write down all the emotions, even if they feel ugly.
- How does the resentment and anger hold me back in my life?
- What do I need to forgive myself for?
- What are some ways I can be kinder and more loving to myself?
- What areas in my life are being affected by my anger?
- What past events have caused me pain or made me afraid to trust others?

These are just a few to get you started. Once you journal for a while, you will reach for your journal whenever you need to express yourself. Your journal should become that perfect best friend who will keep your every secret.

You can use your journal to track your progress. When you make a breakthrough, journal about it, mark the page, and celebrate your progress. Marking your progress and celebrating it are vital because they help you realize your ability to change. You've got this!

## THE ROLE OF COMMUNICATION IN FORGIVING OTHERS

Two types of communication are beneficial for the process of forgiveness. They are direct and indirect. The first is where you speak with the person who caused you pain. You work it out and express your forgiveness to them directly. The second method is for situations where it might be impossible or inadvisable for you to speak to the person. You can either write them a letter and send it to them or write a letter purely for yourself and either keep it or burn it as a way of releasing them and the pain.

Here are some steps and phrases that can help you express forgiveness.

**1. Acknowledge the wrongdoing:**

A. Start by acknowledging the specific action or behavior that hurt you. This shows that you are aware of what happened.

B. Example: "I know what happened [describe the situation] was hurtful."

### 2. Express your feelings:

**A.** Share your emotions without blaming or accusing. Use "I" statements to focus on your feelings.

**B.** Example: "I felt [describe your emotions] when [explain the situation]."

### 3. Declare your decision to forgive:

**A.** Clearly state that you have chosen to forgive the person. Be genuine and clear that you are letting go of all resentment and anger.

**B.** Example: "After reflecting on it, I want you to know I have decided to forgive you."

### 4. Explain your reasons for forgiveness:

**A.** If you feel comfortable, you can explain why you have chosen to forgive. This can help the other person understand your perspective.

**B.** Example: "I believe in the importance of [explain your values or beliefs], and for that reason, I choose to forgive you."

### 5. Offer reassurance:

**A.** Let the person know if you are willing to move forward and rebuild the relationship. Remember that this is not always necessary or even a good idea, depending on the situation.

**B.** Example: "I hope we can move past this and work toward rebuilding our relationship."

## 6. Use positive language:

**A.** Frame your forgiveness message in a positive light to promote healing and reconciliation.

**B.** Example: "I believe in second chances and want us to move forward positively."

## 7. Avoid bringing up the past:

**A.** Once you've expressed your forgiveness, avoid reopening old wounds or dwelling on past mistakes.

**B.** Example: "Let's focus on the present and the positive steps we can take moving forward."

Forgiveness is a personal choice, and the process may vary depending on the situation and individuals involved. It's essential to be genuine and communicate with empathy and understanding. Respecting the other person's boundaries is essential, as you need them to respect yours. Even if you don't understand how they feel, you need to remind yourself that emotions don't have to "make sense" to you; they should at first be validated, but then you need to move on to finding the root cause of them. In this way, you don't dismiss how the other person feels but don't allow the emotional response to be the focus of the discussion.

## NAVIGATING DIFFICULT CONVERSATIONS

When discussing an uncomfortable topic, such as when one person injured another, navigating the situation and knowing where to begin can be difficult. You could approach the meeting with notes you've prepared so you don't get off-topic or forget to address specific points. You must decide whether this method will work with the other party or offend them. Some people may see this as overly formal, especially if you are in a close relationship. You can explain that you want to make sure you are fair and discuss things without allowing emotion to take over the discussion.

Another way to approach the discussion is to give the other person the floor. Ask them to explain what happened from their point of view and then explain the reasoning behind their actions. Sometimes, that alone can help dissipate a lot of the hurt. Many disagreements come from misunderstanding the other person's motives or desires.

While the other party is explaining themselves, practice active listening instead of just waiting for your turn to speak. You can then summarize what they said back to them in your own words to ensure you've understood. Then, you can explain the situation from your point of view and how their actions hurt you.

Sometimes, this is all it takes to end the situation. In many cases, though, the other party won't even come to the table to begin with, and you will have to discover other ways to approach the process of forgiveness.

## MEDITATION AND MINDFULNESS: CULTIVATING INNER PEACE

One of the main reasons for choosing the path of forgiveness is to attain a more peaceful state of mind and life. Let me explain.

You want your mind to rest. But when you attempt to meditate, your mind will do anything but rest. You may struggle against it and eventually give up. I have spoken to many people who have said, "I tried meditating once. It didn't work for me." Meditation isn't something you can "try" and then give up on believing it didn't work. It's like getting in the driver's seat of a car for the first time with no experience, crashing the car, and then saying the car is defective, so you'll never drive again.

As with anything worth doing, you need to be willing to commit. This entire book is about committing to forgiveness. We live in an instant-gratification society, which is not conducive to true peace and mindfulness. It's not something we can "do;" it's something we work toward.

Things like Yoga, journaling, meditation, art, and writing, to name a few, are considered a practice. You never arrive. Many people fail to start a meditation practice because of one simple thing. They don't understand the concept. They think they should be able to master it the first time they start. If I had believed that I never would have continued. I knew meditation would help me because I'd read about many others who testified to their success by meditating. I understood that it would be hard work. I had done the same with other things and wasn't afraid of commitment. I began. And it was hard sometimes. Other times, it was effortless. There was no rhyme or reason why one session would be easy and the other almost impossible.

One of the first lessons I learned to apply to meditation was non-judgment. You have to stop judging. It's not a good session or a terrible session. It's just a session. You might have struggled with too many thoughts or distractions, but that's a symptom and should not be judged. Once you understand this concept, you will find it much easier to relax with your practice. If you approach it without expectation or judgment, you can ease into it and enjoy the benefits, even when it doesn't go exactly how you might wish.

Below, I have listed some different types of meditation. You can do whatever you feel compelled to that day or take a month or more to practice a specific style. It's up to you. No judgment.

### 1. Loving-Kindness Meditation (Metta):

A. This style of meditation is one of the most powerful when you're working toward forgiveness. Metta Meditation aims to send positive feelings and energy toward others or yourself. You can use this to help yourself feel better or to feel empathy toward the person who wronged you. It's powerful, and I would encourage you to try it. It has helped many people on the path to forgiveness.

**B.** How to do Metta Meditation:

a. Find a quiet and comfortable space to sit.

b. Begin by focusing on your breath to calm the mind.

c. Imagine sending yourself feelings of love and kindness and gradually extending those feelings to others, including those you may be in conflict with.

d. Repeat phrases like "May you/I be happy, may you/I be healthy, may you/I be safe, may you/I be at ease."

## 2. Mindful Breathing With Forgiveness:

**A.** Sit in a comfortable position and focus on your breath.

**B.** As you inhale, imagine breathing in positive energy and forgiveness.

**C.** As you exhale, release any negative emotions or grudges. Repeat to yourself: "These feelings of (negative emotion) don't serve me anymore," and replace it with a positive thought.

**D.** Visualize letting go of resentment with each breath.

### 3. Body Scan With Release:

**A.** Lie or sit comfortably, and focus on different body parts, starting from your toes and moving up to your head.

**B.** As you focus on each body part, notice any tension or discomfort.

**C.** With each exhale, visualize releasing the tension and letting go of any negative emotions stored in that part of your body.

### 4. R.A.I.N. Meditation (Recognize, Accept, Investigate, Non-Identification):

**A.** Recognize. Acknowledge and recognize the emotions you're experiencing.

**B.** Accept. Accept that these emotions are present without judgment.

**C.** Investigate. Explore the emotions and their underlying causes with curiosity and compassion.

**D.** Non-Identification. Understand that these emotions do not define you; let go of attachment to them.

Remember, consistency is vital in meditation practice. Experiment with these techniques and find what resonates best with you. Even if you only do one, that is fine; repetition is critical. Over time, they can help cultivate feelings of forgiveness, compassion, and the ability to let go.

## THE ART OF LETTING GO

Letting go is one of the most challenging practices we can undertake. Why is it so difficult for humans to let go? I believe it's because we don't like to give up control. Letting go is precisely that. It is acknowledging that we have no control and actively giving it up.

Earlier, we discussed physical rituals to release situations that no longer serve us. One of the best ways to create a ritual is to follow your intuition. Like my friend who threw a special stone into the river to release the relationship she was struggling to let go, you can find something significant to you that might be good to release.

Objects not only hold memories but carry energy. The person may have left some of their energy behind in that object. Sometimes, we can't understand why we continue to feel attachment to someone when we desire to release them. If there is something of theirs in your home, it may be that the person's energy is causing you to struggle.

Smudging your home and opening the front door to release stale or negative energy can also help. Burning sage has been scientifically proven to clean bacteria in the air, so even if you don't believe it can clear energy, you can at least freshen up your home!

One of the most beneficial rituals is burning. You write what you want to release on paper and then burn the paper with intention. You can then either flush the ashes or, once they are cooled, take them to the forest and release them. There are many ways to perform this ritual, so do what feels right. It doesn't have to be performed in a specific way; what feels good to you will benefit you most.

\* \* \*

Amy had enough. She had gone through so many breakups and men mistreating her that she had decided she wouldn't date anymore until the universe brought her the right man, one who would treat her as she deserved.

To show her commitment to her new path, Amy sat down with a piece of paper and a pen and wrote all her relationship issues on the paper until she'd filled all the space. Then she took a metal bowl from the cupboard and burned the paper. As Amy watched it burn, she imagined all those relationship issues going up in smoke. She released them all and determined to herself that she would do better. After the ashes cooled, Amy walked outside and spread the ashes under a tree as she again imagined the issues floating away in the breeze. When Amy walked back inside her house, she felt light and free.

Several months later, a man asked Amy out on a date. She felt he seemed nice, but she wasn't sure if she was ready. They went out and discovered they had much in common. He was good-looking, kind, and quite interested in her. Amy went on several dates and found herself falling for him. She was afraid she was in for another relationship failure but remembered how she'd released all the old patterns and actively pursued a new way. Amy decided to keep going forward and trust that he was a good man while keeping her eyes open for red flags. Amy and her man have now been together many years, and while they have had to work on things, as in all relationships, she is happy and content. Amy says releasing the old was the best thing she ever did.

*  *  *

You can also write your intentions down on paper and bury them, like burying a seed. Symbolism can help you release or send out an intention. These powerful methods help us mark a specific time and intention that we can look back on.

Visualization is another powerful method of release. Whatever method you choose, make sure it works for you. We are all different, so something that resonates with one person might not work for you, and that's perfectly fine. That's why there are different methods, so you can choose one that works.

## A VISUALIZATION EXERCISE

You can read this over and then begin. Close your eyes. Please take a deep breath and let it out slowly through your nose. Repeat this two more times. When you feel relaxed, begin to see the person you are trying to forgive. Imagine the whole thing, seeing it as clearly as possible and allowing the feelings to fill you. You might be feeling anger, sadness, or several emotions. Try not to get caught up in them, but only observe. Notice what you're feeling. Notice how the situation hurt and angered you. Be the observer.

Now, visualize yourself approaching the person who hurt you. Take their hand in yours and look into their eyes. Say to them, "You hurt me, and I have been so angry at you. But I'm taking back my power today and releasing you. I will no longer allow you to hurt me." Let go of their hand and say, "I forgive you. I forgive you not because what you did was okay or right, it wasn't, but because I deserve better. I deserve to be free. I know you were hurt, which is why you hurt me, but you must figure out your own life. I'm taking my power back from you." Then, visualize the scene slowly fading, the person getting smaller and smaller. The scene gets washed out by a beautiful bright yellow light. This light fills you with joy and peace and fills your entire being. Allow yourself to bask in the glow for a while. Enjoy the peace and lightness you feel from being released from the chains of anger and bitterness. Take several deep breaths, and when you're ready, open your eyes.

### Forgiveness Affirmations

- I am ready to forgive and be free.
- I refuse to allow resentment to control me.
- Gratitude is the way forward.
- I make mistakes, but I will learn from them.
- I deserve healing.
- I will have empathy for others.
- I dare to change my life.
- Forgiveness is about me.
- I am letting go of the past.

These are just a few that you can start with, but it will be even more potent if you create your own. Repeat them to yourself daily, write them in your journal, and empower them with intention.

## RELEASE CONTROL TO FIND IT

Many truths in life are the opposite of what you might expect. For example, the only way to find actual control is to stop trying to control. When you refuse to grant forgiveness, you might think you have control, but you've been giving control to the person you refuse to forgive. When you decide (the key word here is *decide*) to forgive, you take control of the situation and your life.

You are only ever able to control yourself anyway. Anything you thought you were controlling was only an illusion. That illusion was keeping you in chains. Take control of your life now and let forgiveness flow!

## FORGIVING IN LAYERS: UNDERSTANDING THE PROCESS

Forgiving isn't a one-and-done process. Unfortunately, it's more like layers of an onion. You might find more anger and hurt below the surface every time you forgive. Sometimes, the hurt has been piled up layer upon layer in different situations and when you were in different stages of growth in your life. As a result, you may have reacted to the hurt in various ways. Humans are complicated, and healing isn't only a logical process. It takes time and sometimes feels like one step forward, two steps back. It's vital to have patience, as pushing yourself may cause you to struggle and even become blocked. Healing can be a slow process; sometimes, it can seem like you have a sudden change after a long struggle. It's a unique process for everyone, so don't feel you must follow a script.

I remember many years ago, I was struggling with healing over a particular part of my childhood. I read a book, and it was like the lights went on. It all made such sense to me, and over a few weeks, I would read a chapter, put it away, and process what I'd read. By the time I'd finished the book, it felt like I'd come leaps and bounds. I remember waking up one morning and saying, "It's over." It wasn't that I had no more healing to do, but that particular issue had been resolved inside me. This was an example of how healing can go quickly, but it's not the norm. Other things I've worked on have taken years. That is entirely normal, so be kind to yourself and allow the process the time it needs.

Each time you address a new hurt, old feelings of betrayal and anger might arise. This is also completely normal, and you should expect it. As you did before, you should allow the feelings to arise, notice them, and then release them. As you continue to do this, the feelings will be less intense. You can think of them like a small child that wants your attention, and when it gets noticed, it relaxes and goes off to do its own thing.

## THE HEALING POWER OF EMPATHY: SEEING THE OTHER SIDE

Empathy is one of the most powerful traits you can use for yourself and others. We've discussed empathy quite a bit so far, but what is empathy, and how does it differ from sympathy?

**Empathy** is the ability to understand and even share another person's feelings. When you empathize with someone, you walk in their shoes, understanding their feelings and, thus, their motivations.

**Sympathy**, in contrast, is feeling sorry or bad for another person's situation while not necessarily feeling their feelings or understanding their motivations. Sympathy is more about your perspective, while empathy allows you to step into the other person's perspective.

When you use empathy to help you to heal, it is a powerful tool. You can step outside yourself and view your feelings and motivations as you would another person, having compassion and understanding for your process. It's a way of allowing yourself the time to heal without judging yourself or your progress. It's powerful!

Using empathy for the person who wronged you can be challenging, but it is also a powerful tool in the healing process. Again, having empathy and understanding how they have been hurt, which has determined their actions, doesn't mean condoning them in any way. We all do wrong things. That's a fact of life. So, when someone wrongs you, understanding this can help you to step back from the situation and ask yourself what might have caused them to do what they did. Then, you can go even further and step into their shoes, feel the feelings they might have had, and then be able to see their motivations. This is possible even in a case where the person or people did something horrendous, like my uncle's murder. Having empathy for the ones who stole his life was probably one of the most difficult and yet most freeing things I've ever done. I can attest to the fact that it is possible, and it is worth it. It's up to you if you want to be free.

If you find it difficult to empathize with the person who wronged you, you can use your journal to assist you. You can sit down with your journal and write the person's story and imagine how their life may have gone for them to act the way they did. If you don't know their story, imagining it can help you to see things from their perspective. It doesn't matter if you know their actual story; writing down what you think may have happened is a great way to "walk in their shoes" for a while. You could also spend time meditating to visualize them and their possible story. If you know their story, you could allow yourself to walk through it as though you are them and imagine how you would feel if all those things happened to you.

Finding ways to apply empathy will also serve you in other areas of your life. If you can live every day with empathy, it will help you be a kinder, more loving person, and that is never a bad thing. The world can always use more kind and loving people.

### Perspective-Taking Exercise

Choose someone in your life or imagine someone in a hypothetical situation. Spend some time contemplating their experiences, emotions, and perspectives. Try to see the world from their point of view, considering their background, feelings, and challenges. This exercise helps you better understand others' emotions and fosters empathy by encouraging you to step into their shoes.

### Active Listening Practice:

Engage in conversations with others, focusing on being an active listener. Pay close attention to their words, tone, and body language.

Avoid interrupting and resist the urge to formulate your response while they are speaking. Reflect on what you've heard to ensure understanding and ask clarifying questions. Active listening helps build a connection and shows that you value and respect the other person's perspective, fostering empathy.

***Storytelling and Shared Experiences:***

Encourage people around you to share their personal stories, experiences, or challenges. Listen attentively and openly to their narratives without judgment. Share your own stories, fostering a sense of mutual understanding and vulnerability. Recognizing shared human experiences helps break down barriers and builds empathy as you connect with others on a deeper level.

Remember, empathy is a skill that can be developed over time with practice and a genuine willingness to understand others.

## HOW TO REBUILD TRUST

Trust, once lost, is one of the hardest things to get back. If you would like to rebuild trust with the person who injured you, especially if they desire to make amends and gain your trust once more, you should proceed with caution. However, if you feel they are genuine about gaining back your trust, then there are some steps you can take to protect yourself.

### Set Firm Boundaries

If the person truly wants to gain your trust, they will respect any boundaries you have set for the relationship. Regaining trust is a privilege, and the person needs to understand that your boundaries are there to protect you and the relationship and guard against further violations. Be transparent and open with your communication and firm with your boundaries. If you feel them encroaching, communicate with them immediately and make sure they understand they need to step back from the boundary they are approaching, or they risk losing all chance of regaining your trust.

### Clear, Open Communication

Clear communication is vital to regaining the trust that has been lost. You should explain to the other person what they did to lose your trust and what steps they can take to regain it. If they truly desire this, they will show you they are sorry and want to fix things. If not, you have your answer and should be cautious about trusting them. Trust is not a given in all relationships. You must use good judgment to protect yourself but be careful not to become distrustful because that will make it difficult for you to have any successful relationships. You should trust them until the person shows they can't be trusted. However, with all new relationships, you should exercise caution until you know more about the person. Here is a clear plan you can use when reforging lost trust:

## 1. Acknowledgment and Acceptance

- **Step 1:** Acknowledge the breach. Recognize and admit that trust has been broken.
- **Step 2:** Accept responsibility. If you are responsible for the breach, take ownership of your actions.

## 2. Open Communication

- **Step 3:** Initiate honest communication. Express your willingness to rebuild trust through open dialogue.
- **Step 4:** Active listening. Allow the other party to share their feelings, concerns, and expectations without interruption.

## 3. Define Expectations

- **Step 5:** Mutual understanding. Clarify each other's expectations moving forward.
- **Step 6:** Establish boundaries. Clearly define acceptable behaviors and set boundaries to prevent future breaches.

## 4. Create an Action Plan

- **Step 7:** Collaborative planning. Develop a concrete action plan outlining steps to rebuild trust.
- **Step 8:** Realistic goals. Set achievable milestones within a reasonable timeframe.

## 5. Consistent Transparency

- **Step 9:** Full disclosure. Be transparent about your actions, decisions, and intentions.
- **Step 10:** Regular updates. Keep the other party informed of your progress, setbacks, and any changes in the plan.

## 6. Demonstrate Change

- **Step 11:** Behavioral changes. Implement the agreed-upon actions consistently.
- **Step 12:** Learn from mistakes. Demonstrate personal growth by committing to learning from past errors.

## 7. Patience and Understanding

- **Step 13:** Recognize emotions. Rebuilding trust takes time, and emotions may fluctuate.
- **Step 14:** Patience and resilience. Be patient and resilient, maintaining a positive attitude despite setbacks.

## 8. Regular Check-ins

- **Step 15:** Scheduled reviews. Establish regular check-ins to assess progress and address concerns.
- **Step 16:** Open door policy. Encourage open communication at any time, creating a culture of transparency.

### 9. Celebrate Milestone

- **Step 17:** Acknowledge achievements. Celebrate small victories and milestones in rebuilding.
- **Step 18:** Reinforce positive behavior. Positive reinforcement for consistent, trustworthy actions.

### 10. Long-term Maintenance

- **Step 19:** Integration into daily life. Ensure the rebuilt trust becomes integral to your ongoing interactions.
- **Step 20:** Continuous improvement. Commit to ongoing self-reflection and improvement to maintain trust over the long term.

Trust is fragile, and the process may vary based on the severity of the breach. It's crucial to approach the rebuilding process with sincerity, humility, and a genuine desire to repair the relationship.

## CELEBRATING SMALL VICTORIES IN THE JOURNEY OF FORGIVENESS

When you celebrate your victories, no matter how small, you allow yourself to feel your progress. It helps when you feel frustrated and think you aren't getting anywhere or when you suffer a setback. One of the best ways to ensure you don't forget the progress you've made is to write it down in your journal and regularly read over your entries. If you date each entry, it's even easier to remember how far you've come.

You may feel your lack of progress at times, but remember, a day with less anger, a little less sadness, or even finding that you're not thinking about the situation or person as much is a lot of progress! Remember to have empathy for yourself and congratulate yourself on all progress, no matter how small it may seem. Those little things add up quickly to a happier, more peaceful life.

Milestones are a great way to mark your progress. You could set some milestones for yourself that feel achievable, such as

- meditating for 10 minutes without distraction.
- going half a day without thinking negative thoughts about yourself or the other person(s).
- spending a day doing something special for yourself.
- writing in your journal for a whole week without missing a day.
- having gratitude daily.
- making peace with the situation (this is a big one!).
- having an open conversation with the person who injured you and making peace with them.

When you have victories, you should share them with supportive people in your life. It helps to feel proud of yourself for what you've accomplished. When you're feeling down, you can remember how you felt when you shared those victories, and your friends and family can remind you of them as well.

Remember, gratitude is the way forward. When you are grateful for what you have, the things you don't have or those that were taken away aren't at center stage in your mind. Gratitude is a beautiful way to deal with the ups and downs of life. It's like focusing on the silver lining in every situation. When you do that, you will be surprised at how many good things are right before you. One thing I like to say to myself:

**What you think about, you bring about.**

When you focus on positive things, you bring more of that into your life. When you focus on the negative, the same is true. The universe wants to give you what you want. If you think about everything you don't have, the universe will keep you in the same state. The universe doesn't differentiate between positive and negative; it just fulfills your deepest desires. So, remember, what you think about all the time is what you'll get more of. Focus on plenty, gratitude, and everything you want to see in your life, and you'll receive more.

### One Caveat

The universe doesn't value the things we do. Money and things are just that. We all know by now that money doesn't make us happy. The wealthiest people in the world are often the most miserable and lonely. So be careful not to get caught up in the "I'll think about money all the time, and I'll be rich." You might. And if you do, you might lose everything that matters in life. So, live with intention. Your intention should be to be rich in family, friends, and love. The rest are just the things that make us more physically comfortable.

## ESTABLISHING HEALTHY BOUNDARIES POST FORGIVENESS

Once you've reached the place where you've released the hurt and anger, you must ensure you set up healthy boundaries to guard yourself from being in that place again. It won't stop situations from happening, but it can allow you to see it happening and take steps to move away from the place where you'll be injured. Boundaries are like warning signs.

Think of cities of old, before we had digital warning systems to guard us. There would be a city with thick walls to keep intruders out. But usually, they also had guard posts or even an outer wall to keep the intruders even farther back. The guard posts were early warning systems of intrusion, and they gave the city time to pull back and prepare for invasion.

That's what boundaries are far. They are a warning system that someone is pushing too far into your life and disrespecting your limits. When they hit your outer boundaries, this is a signal to you that you need to pull back and warn them off.

Diana was new on the dating scene. She was married for over twenty-five years when her husband passed away. She had finished the grieving process and was ready to meet someone new. She had no experience, but her best friend said she should set up a dating profile. She did and was shocked at the response. Before long, she met a man who seemed nice. He said and did all the right things, but something felt off to Diana. She agreed to go on another date, but while they were having dinner, he began asking her about her life and whether she was dating other people. She felt the questions were a bit intrusive, but she answered.

Later that week, she went on a date with another man. While at the restaurant, she thought she saw Dan, the man she'd seen a couple of times, at the back of the restaurant watching her and her date. Diana got prickles down her spine and felt very uncomfortable. She carried on with the date. She kept looking around but didn't see him again.

When Diana arrived home, she checked her phone, as she always kept it off on dates. She found fifteen messages from Dan. He didn't say he'd been at the restaurant but asked her where she was, why she wasn't answering, etc. Diana knew this man had a problem and could see he didn't respect her boundaries. She didn't respond to him and blocked him on her profile. She was grateful that she hadn't let him know where she lived. But his being at the restaurant worried her, as he might be following her. She took steps to protect herself, and on new dates, she was more careful not to respond when she felt someone crossing her boundaries and wanting to know too much information about her.

* * *

## THE IMPORTANCE OF SELF-CARE IN THE FORGIVENESS JOURNEY

If you're an empath, you might have difficulty with boundaries. Being an empath means you feel what others feel almost all the time. It can be challenging because it can feel like your mission in the world is to help others heal their pain. One of the first things you need to learn as an empath is to protect yourself and your energy. If you don't, many people will take your energy for themselves. You have to learn to care for yourself first before caring for others. If you keep giving without replenishing yourself, you will have nothing left. That is why boundaries are so important, especially for empaths.

Even for those who aren't empaths, self-care is vital. It's like they say on a plane when giving the safety demonstration. You must put on your mask before helping others. Self-care is the same. If you don't ensure your needs are met, you won't be able to assist others and certainly won't be able to give them your best care.

Self-care means taking care of your needs. That's your emotional, physical, and mental needs. Everyone has different needs, so spend time thinking and maybe journaling about what makes you feel rested and cared for. For me, it's time alone. I will have a bath and read a book. Or spend time outside in nature. I might go to the spa and get a pedicure. I will also spend time journaling and writing or reading. These things help me to replenish because I'm an introvert. Others, maybe more extroverted people, need time with others, like good friends or family. They might need to go out and drink with a friend or dance. That's why I say we all have different needs, and self-care will look different to each of us.

If you struggle to do self-care, maybe you need to spend some time journaling about it or seek a therapist to discover why. Many of us struggle with it because when we were children, we weren't given the space to care for ourselves or didn't see our parents partaking in self-care. Or we were abused and told we didn't deserve anything good. These things can be reasons we don't care for ourselves, but they must be addressed if you have any of these issues. Self-care is a vital part of living a healthy, positive life. You may struggle with the forgiveness journey if you don't have these things. How can you be free from resentment and anger if you don't feel you deserve to be cared for?

If you don't care for yourself, your body will reveal it. You might have tension in your shoulders, headaches, or even ailments with no cause. These can all indicate a need for self-care for your emotional well-being.

* * *

When Jeanette was young, her mother would criticize her constantly. It seemed that no matter what Jeanette did, she was wrong. Over time, and even into her adulthood, she would have headaches almost daily. She saw her doctor, but he could find no physical cause. She hated having to take medicine all the time, so she went to see a massage therapist. He told her that her muscles were bunched up in her neck and helped to relax them. But within days after the appointment, the headaches and tension were back.

On most weekdays, Jeanette would call her mother and chat so she could check up on her. Jeanette's mother would complain and then find fault with something in her daughter or tell her she hadn't done something she was asked to do. It drove Jeanette crazy. After many visits to the massage therapist, Jeanette began to notice that her tension would come back as soon as she got on the phone with her mother. She realized that the source of her headaches wasn't physical but emotional. Her mother was continuing the abuse she'd given Jeanette as a child. It was time for something to change.

Jeanette told her mother she would no longer allow her to criticize and be mean to her. She began to say goodbye and hung up the phone the minute the barrage started. She wasn't rude, just firm. She knew it was time for her to have boundaries with her mother. At first, her mother was furious, but over time, she began to realize if she wanted a relationship with her daughter, she would need to be kinder. It took time, but they soon built a better relationship. Jeanette's headaches went away, and she no longer needed to see a massage therapist. Instead, she began to see a therapist to deal with her childhood trauma so she could heal and forgive her mother.

* * *

Proper self-care takes all of you into account—your body, mind, and soul. To be free and healthy, you must keep self-care a part of your life and never neglect yourself. The forgiveness journey isn't just about forgiving one incident; it's about living a life free from anger and resentment. It's about living your best, most successful life. So, caring for yourself is another part of the process. Think about how good you'll feel if you regularly meet your needs. You'll be relaxed, stress-free, and living the life you deserve to live!

# CHAPTER 4

# THE DECISION TO INTEGRATE FORGIVENESS INTO DAILY LIFE

## DAILY AFFIRMATIONS TO FOSTER FORGIVENESS

You can use daily affirmations to keep your mind on the path of forgiveness. You can craft them yourself or look up ones on the internet that resonate with you. There are also books of affirmations you can use to assist you. You can create some of your own affirmations by using prompts from this list:

- I forgive myself for…
- I let go of resentment for …
- The past is not my future, and I will…
- My mistakes are only mistakes, and I forgive myself for…
- I deserve happiness despite…
- I forgive… for…

You can craft some daily affirmations that you can write in your journal and say aloud to yourself to combat negative thoughts. That can be one of the most significant challenges on the forgiveness road. Negative thoughts can quickly undo many months of work. Keep a reign on those thoughts with positive affirmations.

While you are waiting in lines, driving to work, or doing housework, your mind will wander. Pay attention to the thoughts running through your mind and use the affirmations to help keep your thoughts positive. Using the time when your mind isn't busy with work or doing something meaningful is the perfect way to remind yourself of your goals.

Positive affirmations can help you keep moving forward on your path to forgiveness, elevate your self-esteem, and deepen your capacity for forgiveness in all areas of your life.

## THE ROLE OF GRATITUDE IN A FORGIVING LIFE

When you choose gratitude as your foundation, it improves all areas of your life. Rather than focusing on the hurts, big or small, you focus on the good things in life. We all have struggles and go through pain caused by others, intentionally or unintentionally, but keeping your thoughts on gratitude is helpful to keep yourself from allowing the hurts to fester. Gratitude living helps to foster a forgiving heart.

We discussed incorporating gratitude into your daily life through journaling, meditation, and affirmations. You can devise other ways to help yourself focus on gratitude daily and not allow life's hurts and negative experiences to become your only reality.

A gratitude-filled heart will also positively impact your relationships. You will enjoy the people around you and regularly tell them how you feel. This will foster gratitude in them and become a beautiful cycle of love and appreciation.

## OVERCOMING BARRIERS WITH GRATITUDE

My sister Kelly was entangled in a web of resentment and hurt after a profound betrayal. Sleepless nights were filled with echoes of past wounds until she stumbled upon a book about gratitude. Kelly decided to embark on a journey to shift her perspective. Each day, she diligently recorded moments of gratitude in her journal, from the warmth of the morning sun to the kindness of a stranger's smile. As the pages filled, a transformation occurred within her. The lens through which she viewed the world widened, and the burden of resentment gradually lifted. The everyday practice of gratitude became a balm for her wounded soul, allowing forgiveness to bloom where bitterness once thrived. Kelly realized that acknowledging the positives in her life brought solace and paved the way for understanding the complexities of human nature. In embracing a gratitude mindset, she discovered the key to unlocking the gates of forgiveness, liberating herself from the pain of the past. The key for her, and so many others, is consistency. Gratitude must be part of your daily life for you to have results.

## FORGIVENESS AND RELATIONSHIPS: NAVIGATING COMPLEX DYNAMICS

Forgiveness isn't just something you do after a huge issue happens. It should be something experienced in everyday life. It's an attitude toward others that makes relationships much easier to navigate. Many people live their lives looking for offense. Another person might say something simple, but they'll take it the wrong way and get offended. If you want to be offended, you will find plenty of opportunities.

On the other hand, if you live with an open heart and understand that people say and do things not intending to hurt you, you will seldom feel offended. And even if they meant to hurt you, you can step back and ask yourself why they might have done so.

Understanding one simple thing can save you from many conflicts: It's not about you. I try to remind myself of this regularly. It's not about me. It's not about you. When a person walks through life and comes into contact with you, their reaction to you is usually more about them, their preconceived notions, and their biases than it has to do with you. Even people who know you well have expectations and biases that have little to do with you. Most people see you as a mirror reflecting what they want or don't want to see. Sometimes, you might even remind them of someone they don't like or who hurt them in the past, so they decide they don't like you.

It's unfair how some people treat you, but you can't change it. So, if you can allow it to pass over you, you will be much happier and less stressed about what others are doing and saying. It doesn't matter what people think of you anyway. It's more important to be your genuine self; the people who connect with you will be the ones you want to have in your life.

When you meet someone who interests you romantically, this is even more important. The things that initially attract people to one another are often the things that break them up. I've wondered why this is. I believe it's because as the romance wears off and reality sets in, we allow the small things to build up, and resentment becomes a wall between the two people. If you, instead, choose to understand that people can be annoying and not allow the annoyance to turn into resentment, you will be able to forgive and be kind to your partner. You will have the best chance of having a long-lasting, happy relationship.

Boundaries are constructive here. If you find yourself bothered by someone's behavior, removing yourself from the situation could be an excellent way to calm down and let it go. If your friend, partner, or whoever won't allow you to remove yourself, some boundary-setting needs to occur. We all have times when we need space, and the people in our lives should be able to respect this without causing an issue. You need to be able to do the same with them.

Communication is vital to restoring harmony when you have a conflict with someone in your life. Many different communication strategies can facilitate mutual understanding.

## 1. Active Listening

**A. Description:** Actively listening involves fully concentrating, understanding, responding, and remembering what the other person is saying.

**B. Implementation:**

a. Give your full attention to the speaker.
b. Make eye contact and use open body language.
c. Avoid interrupting; let the speaker express their thoughts without judgment.
d. Reflect on what you've heard and ask clarifying questions to ensure understanding.

## 2. Empathetic Communication

**A. Description:** Empathy is the ability to understand and share the feelings of another. Empathetic communication acknowledges the other person's emotions and expresses understanding and care.

**B. Implementation:**

a. Acknowledge the other person's emotions without judgment.
b. Use phrases like "I understand how you feel" to convey empathy.
c. Share your feelings to create a sense of mutual vulnerability.
d. Avoid blame and instead focus on expressing empathy and understanding.

### 3. I-Statements for Expressing Feelings

**A. Description:** I-Statements are a communication technique where you express your feelings, thoughts, and needs in a way that emphasizes personal responsibility rather than blaming the other person.

**B. Implementation:**

    a. Begin statements with "I feel" to express emotions.
    b. Clearly state the behavior or situation causing the emotion.
    c. Share the impact the behavior or situation has on you.
    d. Conclude with a request or suggestion for resolution.

Remember, these communication strategies work best when used together and with a genuine intention to understand and forgive. Building trust through effective communication is crucial for a relationship's health and success.

## THE IMPACT OF FORGIVENESS ON PERSONAL GROWTH

*Self-awareness*

One of the benefits of going on this journey of forgiveness is that you should now have greater self-awareness in your life. You better understand your values and strengths and how best to use them. When you see an area in your life that needs to change, you have the skills and understanding to begin the growth process. You understand the tools you have gained to assist you in the new growth process. Self-awareness is a powerful tool in your arsenal.

### Emotional intelligence

Understanding your emotions is called emotional intelligence. It means you understand that they are not permanent, nor should you base decisions on them. At the same time, you understand emotions can't be ignored and have their place in your life. Emotional intelligence means you are now better at regulating your emotions. They don't run your life and aren't all over the place. With emotional intelligence, you have better empathy for others, which assists you in your relationships and helps you continue a forgiving lifestyle.

### Life lessons

You will have learned through this journey that pain is not permanent. When you choose to forgive, you allow the pain to leave you. Some people think that pain is always with you, but it doesn't have to be. You will have learned this on your forgiveness journey. You can take many lessons with you and apply them to other lessons in your life. Life is about learning lessons, so it's wise to understand and learn the lesson as quickly as possible. I have found that when you resist the lesson, it gets more painful. No one wants more pain, but we humans seem to learn best that way. Being resilient and not giving up will help you learn the lesson and move on.

\* \* \*

"Life always seems to kick me when I'm down." Vanessa was known for saying this all the time. It seemed that no matter how things were going, something would happen to bring her down or cause problems in her life. She thought she was unlucky. She would be out with a bunch of friends, and it would be her who would have something go wrong, like losing her wallet or getting food poisoning when everyone else was okay.

Vanessa's best friend, Jenny, would tell her to think positively. She told Vanessa that thinking she was unlucky was causing her to be so. She told Vanessa, "What you think about, you bring about." Vanessa decided to try to change her thinking. It took some time, and she even began journaling and writing positive things daily to remind herself. Eventually, she noticed she no longer felt unlucky and had fewer petty problems. Vanessa realized Jenny was right and determined always to do her best to think positively and bring the best things to her life.

You can change your life by changing your mind. It's a simple sentence, but not as easy to bring about. Choosing the path less traveled is a matter of choice and changing your mindset. As forgiveness unfolds, your perspective on life will shift to feelings of empathy and understanding. Once elusive, happiness will begin to bloom like wildflowers in the most unexpected places. This profound change in perspective will ripple through every aspect of your life, guiding you toward a newfound sense of purpose and direction. In embracing forgiveness, you will discover it isn't just about releasing the grip on the past; it is about unlocking a future filled with compassion, joy, and a profound understanding of the transformative power of forgiveness.

## RESILIENCE THROUGH FORGIVENESS: BUILDING EMOTIONAL STRENGTH

If you want to build resilience, you can do that through a forgiveness mindset. When you allow the frustrations and things that other people do to you to run off you like water off a duck's back, you build a mindset of forgiveness and aren't so swayed by everything other people do. It's like being an oak tree in a windstorm. Everything can blow and fly around you without knocking you over.

Even after you feel you have completed your forgiveness journey, you can continue to use the same strategies to cope with the trials and challenges of life and the things that other people can throw at you. Remember to journal and meditate regularly to keep yourself open and in the forgiveness mindset. These are some of the most powerful coping strategies you can employ for the rest of your life.

One thing that you can guarantee is that there will be other hurts in the future. No matter how much you might try to keep your distance from people who don't share your mindset, they will show up in your life. Maybe even to test your boundaries or to test your coping strategies. These challenging people will test you for whatever reason, so it's important to remember everything you've learned on this journey. They will be the skills that help you most.

* * *

Work had been demanding that day, and Greg dragged his feet as he entered the restaurant area of the resort, where he worked to pick up his family's supper for the evening. He only wanted to get to his room and relax with his wife and daughter. Just as Greg picked up the tray, he heard footsteps behind him. His heart sank at the thought of the inevitable confrontation, and he braced himself.

"Your wife didn't bring back the dishes from last night. I need all the trays!" Amara snapped at him, her mean face filled with out-of-proportion vitriol, considering the pettiness of the situation.

Greg resisted and looked at the pile of trays sitting on the counter. There weren't even any guests at the resort yet, and Amara didn't need the trays back that minute; she just needed to complain. He never came into the kitchen without being criticized, usually for something petty. Amara seemed to take pleasure in bothering him as much as possible. He knew she had a miserable heart and that it was pointless to fight with her, but at the same time, he objected to disrespect. Greg was a hard worker, always trying to do his best and keep his head down. But no matter what he did or how well, there was always a problem, and every time he was around Amara, she tried to make him feel bad about himself.

"She wasn't feeling well, Amara; I will bring the trays and dishes back in the morning." Greg kept a lid on his temper even though it boiled beneath the surface like a volcano eager to erupt.

"Well, make sure they're back in the morning," she snapped as she huffed out of the room. Greg rolled his eyes and sighed as he left the kitchen.

\* \* \*

No matter how much Greg tried to be kind and let the disrespect go, it made no difference. You'll meet people who choose to be miserable because you've learned by now it's a choice and not something that just happens to you. There will always be challenges in life, but it's your choice how you respond to them. A positive mindset is not easy, but anything worth having is worth the work.

Continuous practice of a positive mindset and using tools, such as journaling, are important to maintaining peace of mind and a forgiveness focus. It's too easy to fall back into old patterns, and this way, you can safeguard yourself against that.

## FORGIVENESS AND LETTING GO OF THE PAST

Keeping old hurt around and in your mind is a burden. You have chosen to lay that burden down, and you should feel lighter. Be careful to avoid picking it up again or even creating a new one. Here are some ways to release the past and keep yourself from creating new burdens.

**Acknowledgment**

- **Step 1:** Recognize the Grievance

  ○ Acknowledge and identify the specific incident or situation that has caused pain or resentment.

- **Step 2:** Accept Emotional Impact

  ○ Allow yourself to feel the emotions associated with the grievance without judgment.

**Understanding**

- **Step 3:** Reflect on Perspectives

  ○ Consider the perspectives of all parties involved, recognizing that people may have different views and motivations.

- **Step 4:** Empathize With Intentions

  ○ Try to understand the intentions behind the actions, acknowledging that people make mistakes or act out of ignorance.

**Acceptance**

- **Step 5:** Embrace Imperfections

  ○ Recognize the imperfections in yourself and others, understanding that everyone is fallible.

- **Step 6:** Release the Need for Control

  ○ Let go of the desire to control outcomes or change the past. Accept that some things are beyond your control.

## Release

- **Step 7:** Choose Forgiveness

  ○ Make a conscious decision to forgive. Understand that forgiveness does not condone actions but frees one from the burden of resentment.

- **Step 8:** Release Negative Attachments

  ○ Practice detachment from negative emotions associated with the grievance. This may involve forgiveness exercises, meditation, or therapeutic techniques.

- **Step 9:** Create a Symbolic Act

  ○ Consider a symbolic gesture or ritual that represents letting go, such as writing a letter and burning it, symbolizing the release of the grievance.

**Moving Forward**

- **Step 10:** Focus on the Present

  - Redirect your energy toward the present and future rather than dwelling on the past.

- **Step 11:** Establish Boundaries

  - Set clear boundaries to prevent a recurrence of similar grievances, ensuring healthy relationships moving forward.

- **Step 12:** Cultivate Positive Growth

  - Use the experience as an opportunity for personal growth, learning, and cultivating resilience.

## ENVISIONING A FUTURE UNBURDENED BY THE PAST

Imagine a life unburdened by anger and resentment. Imagine feeling light and happy and enjoying all life has to offer. It won't be a life free from problems, but it can be one where you can control your reactions and set and maintain healthy boundaries. This is the place we are working toward through the path of forgiveness.

Setting goals for yourself can help you get to the place I've described above, and it can also help you maintain that peaceful life. In your journal, you can list what you value and want to achieve and how you will do it. You have worked hard to get to this point, and I'm sure you don't want to return to how things were. You must ensure you are keeping to your boundaries and doing your self-care rituals to keep your mind and body healthy. When you are tired and not feeling well, it is tempting to ease up on your boundaries and let your self-care lapse. You mustn't do that. All of these things are important and must become a part of your daily life if you're going to maintain your healthy outlook and reach your goals.

This path you've chosen will not only have wonderful results in your life but also be a legacy you can leave to your children and an example to your friends and family. You don't even have to tell them what you're doing; they will see the results in your positive outlook, your changed attitude, and your new boundaries. They may even ask you what you've done to change so much. I know; it's happened to me.

Remember, if you're not growing, you're dying. It's that simple. Human beings don't stagnate. If you're not moving forward, you're going backward. Keep yourself in a growth state by reading books that help you grow in other areas, taking a course in something that interests you, or starting a new hobby. There are many ways to keep growing in your life. Meeting new people and forming healthy, fun relationships is another way. Find what works for you and put all your effort into creating a healthy, happy life. You've got this!

## FORGIVENESS IN DIFFERENT CULTURES

Different cultures view forgiveness and that mindset in different ways. Western cultures tend to have a more individualistic mindset, which means they often put the needs of the individual ahead of the needs of the group. That could be family, friends, or workmates. Other countries, like Asia and Africa, have a more collectivistic culture that puts the group's needs before the individual. So, if a person is offended or hurt by someone in the group, they might more easily distance themselves from the person and group and keep the hurt to themselves rather than communicate and grant forgiveness.

This is a generalization because you can't put all people in a box, but it is generally true of different cultures. Also, immigration will impact cultures as people mix and adopt other cultures' practices.

There are two types of forgiveness implied in this. One is decisional forgiveness, which is more analytical and usually done based on the best outcome for the situation. This might be used in a collectivist culture to keep the group dynamic happy. The other type of forgiveness is emotional forgiveness, which focuses more on the injured party's emotional needs. This is the more common type in individualistic cultures. It focuses more on the person and rarely considers the group dynamic.

> "The question is whether emotional forgiveness follows decisional forgiveness in collectivistic people," says Toussaint. "Something called cognitive dissonance might interfere." In short, it's difficult for people to say one thing and believe another—our brains struggle to allow two contradictory thoughts to exist, and it creates additional psychological stress.

*As a result, if we say we believe something, that belief tends to materialize.*

PARK, 2023.

This is why something like veganism can be a person's life philosophy, not just a diet. Their reasons for not eating meat become a value for them and affect their decisions in all areas of their lives. Similarly, for someone who makes an analytical decision to forgive, the rest of their life will align with that choice. Thus, they will likely also feel emotional satisfaction from that decision. It follows that if you want to be more of a forgiving person, choosing to forgive is the best start.

It's interesting how different cultures view concepts and practice relationship dynamics. Denmark is a Western culture, but the people are more decisional in their approach. Their groups are tight-knit and supportive. Therefore, it makes sense that even though they are a Western society, they might be more about group dynamics than the individual. They have a group of "laws" that children are taught early in life. It's called Jante's law. There are 10, but the first is "You're not to think *you* are anything special." And it goes on in this vein. How would this concept cause us to approach relationships differently? It's not that people don't treat their family and children well; I think they often treat them better with this concept because it also applies to the parents. It's about you not thinking you're above anyone else. Another way of putting it is the Golden Rule: Treat others how you want to be treated. This would go a long way toward people being kinder and less likely to hold grudges.

You can do just one little thing to help you feel better and healthier, reduce stress, and help prevent mental illness. It's saying I forgive you. It's incredible how these three little words can make such a difference in your life, but many cultures understand this and make it a part of their everyday life and cultural sayings.

In Hawaiian culture, they have a saying, "Ho'oponopono," which roughly means, "I am sorry, please forgive me, I love you" (Park, 2023). This is a simplified definition, but it's often difficult to describe a concept outside of the language in which it exists. A culture's language and concepts are taught to people from birth, so a concept like forgiveness, which might be more difficult in Western societies, is much more ingrained in other cultures and is expected.

That's not to say that their way is better or worse; either way presents challenges. In Western culture, I feel people can be held more accountable. If they act a certain way, people will be less likely to stay in a relationship with them. For example, in other cultures, like Greek culture, challenging people can get away with their bad behavior because the family accepts that "that's just how they are." Let's go back to Greg and Amara as an example of this.

* * *

After weeks of working for the Greek family, Greg was almost at the end of his rope. His stomach tied itself in knots every time he went into Amara's area of the resort, the kitchen, and the restaurant. There wasn't a time when he could enter, and she didn't jump down his throat about something. Usually, it was something minor or not even his fault. She picked on anything and everything she could think of.

One day, Greg was working on something in the kitchen, trying to keep out of her way, when he heard Amara's niece, Elena, yelling. He peeked around the corner, shocked to see them both red-faced and screaming at each other. Elena stomped out of the kitchen, rolling her eyes at Greg as she left.

Another time, Maria, Amara's older sister, ranted to Greg about how her sister lorded over all of them. He didn't understand why they didn't speak to her about it, telling her they wouldn't accept her behavior anymore. He asked Maria about it. Greg was from a Western culture, so it was easy for him. If someone mistreats you, you speak to them, and if they don't stop the behavior, you stay away from them. He was stuck in the relationship with Amara because he worked there, but the family had much more power than he did.

He said this to Maria, and she said it was okay; Amara doesn't mean to be like that. Greg stared at her. "What do you mean she doesn't mean to do it? Of course, she does. She's been getting away with it her whole life because no one confronts her and tells her they won't take it from her anymore." Greg felt comfortable talking this way to Maria because they were close, and he knew she respected him for his work ethic and who he was.

"No, Greg, we can't do that. She doesn't know how to say things like us. It's just her way."

Greg felt frustrated because she didn't understand. He'd spoken to Maria a few times about how Amara treated him, but she brushed it off and asked him to let it go. It was getting more and more difficult for him to do so. He didn't believe people should be allowed to treat people that way, but in Greece, that's how things are often done. He had a mindset of immersing himself in the culture of the country he lived in rather than trying to force his values on them, but he had difficulty wrapping his mind around this.

Then came the day his wife was in tears because of something mean and unfair Amara said to her. Greg, furious, confronted Amara. She didn't back down, but the other family members came to him separately to commiserate with him. They said they were sorry Amara was mean to his wife but to please let it go. It infuriated Greg, but what was he to do? He loved his job, but he also loved his wife and hated seeing her hurt that way.

The only solution was for him to either stay out of her way, accept the family's solution, or find another job.

* * *

So, what do the ancient Greeks think of the concept of forgiveness?

For Greeks, to forgive means to let go or release. They also have another word: giving free and unconditional forgiveness. The concept of forgiveness, meaning to release or let go, can be applied not just to the person being forgiven but also to the person doing the forgiving. It's a letting go for both, especially the wounded party.

We can learn much from other cultures, but we also need to apply what we've learned in our own lives. Forgiveness is good for our relationships and our mental health. When we hold onto the feelings caused by the incident, we could hold a grudge, which isn't healthy for our minds or bodies.

When a negative situation occurs, we are affected by all the emotions and pain that arise from it. If we hold on to those feelings long after the incident, that could be considered holding a grudge. Usually, after some time passes, the feelings fade. But other times, you might find it challenging to let go of those feelings, and you might not even be aware you're holding onto them.

Holding a grudge can impact you much more than the person you're angry at. Keeping the anger close might feel like a shield, but it's only hurting you. It's something that children do, but adults are expected to grow out of that behavior, process the emotions, and deal with the situation. Abuse in childhood can stunt the growth of this area of our lives and cause us to remain stuck in this behavior pattern. Examining the issues from the past may help determine if this is the case for you. We all have areas of pain from our childhoods that can cause stunted growth, but when we address them, we can remove that block and begin to grow again and mature in that area.

When you hold onto anger, it allows the anger to fester and produce more anger. It becomes a vicious cycle, and you will find that you get more and more angry, especially as other incidents occur, not even necessarily with the same person. It can set your mind up toward negativity and cause resentment to fester.

Keeping that negative mindset is draining. It's much easier for your mind to have pleasant thoughts because negative thoughts can also cause overthinking, where you replay the events repeatedly and exhaust your mind. Even as time passes, when you continue to replay the events, it will feel like the incident just happened rather than allow the memory to fade and the emotions to recede. This harms your mental health. It takes up space in your mind where better, more positive could exist.

This is self-inflicted, so if you allow yourself to release the anger and resentment and decide to stop holding grudges, you can free yourself from this negative effect on your mind and body.

Holding grudges can affect many systems in your body, such as your

You might experience headaches, struggle with sleeping, or feel nervous in your stomach. All of these things have huge impacts over time. It's up to you to take care of your mental and physical health, so it's vital to deal with any anger issues.

Your mental state can be the determining factor of how peaceful or chaotic your life is. Do yourself a favor and deal with any issues that might disrupt you and cause your health to suffer. You'll be so glad you did!

# CHAPTER 5
# THE TRANSFORMATIVE POWER OF FORGIVENESS

## FORGIVENESS AS A SUPERPOWER: STORIES OF TRANSFORMATION

F orgiveness can truly be a superpower. Understanding how it works and how it can transform your entire life gives you an advantage over many other people—thus, a superpower! Here are some stories of how forgiveness has transformed other lives, even in the midst of chaos and trauma. I hope they inspire you to live your life with the same power!

### Dr. Ahmadi: Trauma Surgeon

War raged all around him, but Dr. Ahmadi believed he could make a difference to the soldiers and the civilians caught up in the violence. With gunfire and explosions all around, Dr. Ahmadi worked tirelessly to repair the damage to his patients' bodies caused by the relentless war machine.

Underneath his calm, stoic face, he raged. The wastefulness of human life, all for a cause most of them didn't even believe in, began to eat away at his belief in making a difference. Every innocent life lost created more havoc in his soul. Before long Dr. Ahmadi found himself filled with anger he struggled to quell with no outlet.

One night, as he headed to his quarters after an exhausting day working in the trauma room, a shadow emerged from the darkness. It was the uniform that first drew his eyes, that of an enemy soldier, but the anguish on his face caused Dr. Ahmadi to stop in his tracks. He examined his uniform and quickly realized it wasn't a common soldier but a general, one whose face his side knew well. The man standing before him was one of the reasons for all of his anger and bitterness. This man's commands sent many of their soldiers, and many of his own, to an early grave.

In that moment, he was faced with a challenge. Would he allow his hatred and anger to send him down the path of violence, or would he embrace the transformative power of forgiveness and reach out with compassion for a fellow human being?

Feeling lighter than he had in many months, Dr. Ahmadi chose forgiveness and helped the enemy general, healing his traumatic wounds and giving him his life back. Dr. Ahmadi could easily have allowed the man to die and maybe turned the tide of the war. The wounds were life-threatening. Without a trauma surgeon nearby, the general would have died within hours.

From that day, Dr. Ahmadi dedicated his life to a path of forgiveness and to healing not only the physical wounds that marred his patients' bodies but also the invisible scars that haunted their souls. After each successful surgery, he took the time to speak with each patient, encouraging them to deal with the anger produced by the trauma to help them heal both inside and out.

His hospital became a sanctuary, a symbol of hope in a region consumed by war. Through his tireless efforts, Dr. Ahmadi proved that forgiveness was not a sign of weakness but a beacon of strength, capable of overcoming any barrier.

### James: Wrongly Imprisoned

James entered the world as a free man after many years behind bars for a crime he didn't commit. Injustice and the trauma of prison life had caused a deep rage inside him, looking for a place to land. James faced a choice that would determine the course of the rest of his life. Would he allow the rage and bitterness of injustice to consume and twist him as so many former prisoners did, or would he forge a new path and be an example of a better way?

It took James several years to wrestle with the demons of his anger. Only after he lost a close friend by exploding his anger over a situation that wasn't the friend's fault was he able to see the path he was on. James decided at that moment that he needed to choose a new path. He called his friend, apologized, and asked for help. He and his friend decided that the only way forward was to forgive the system that had put him behind bars and help others like him. They also decided to help heal the system.

The prison had taken many years of his life, but James knew he had many years left if he didn't waste them on substance abuse and risky behavior as he had since his release. He cleaned himself up and went back to school to become a lawyer. He graduated with honors, respect of his entire class, and the pride of his family.

James and his friend, now partner, Elina, then opened an advocacy practice where they fought for justice for prisoners who had been wrongly imprisoned as he had. James knew that not all the people he fought for were as innocent as he had been, but despite the risk of defending someone who had lied, he knew there were many he was saving. James brought the power of the forgiveness mindset to each person he defended and saw many lives transformed just as he had been. James knew that his true legacy lay not in the years he had lost behind bars but in the lives he had touched and the hearts he had helped to heal along the way.

### Maria: Assault Survivor

Maria's world shattered the night she became a victim of a brutal assault. For Maria, it seemed that her life was over as she battled with depression, fear, and despair. In desperation, she called a former classmate who she knew had gone through a similar experience. Her friend was thrilled that Maria had reached out before it was too late and explained what had helped her through the trauma of her own assault. She'd turned to art therapy.

Maria had been a passionate artist as a child but hadn't painted for many years. She couldn't help but feel that the universe had given her the nudge to call her friend so she would turn to the healing power of art expression. With new paints and canvases ready, Maria, with a tremble in her hand, dipped her brush into the paint and began to express her pain and anguish in a safe place. With every stroke, Maria painted away her anger and pain and discovered a desire to forgive and release herself from the trauma. As Maria spoke with her friend and learned how she had begun to forge a path to forgiveness through art, Maria determined she would do the same.

Through her paintings, Maria found solace, forgiveness, and healing. Every painting became a step on her journey to healing, a testament to her resilience and determination to rise above the ashes of tragedy.

But Maria's story did not end with her healing journey. Driven by a desire to turn her pain into purpose, she became an advocate for survivors of trauma, using her art as a medium to reach those who had also experienced violent trauma.

Through exhibitions and workshops, Maria shared her story with the world, inspiring others to find healing and hope amid their pain. And so, Maria's masterpiece of forgiveness continued to unfold, its colors swirling and shifting with each passing day. Through her art, she healed her wounds. She also inspired compassion and empathy in others, proving that the canvas of forgiveness is a powerful medium for self-expression, healing, and, ultimately, transformation.

These stories showcase the diverse paths to forgiveness, demonstrating that it can be a catalyst for personal growth, resilience, reconciliation, and even societal change. The transformative power of forgiveness is a testament to the human spirit's capacity to rise above adversity and create positive change.

It is the discovery of your transformation from victim to survivor that can be an example to others! When people see a formerly angry person living in peace and contentment, they will ask questions and desire the same transformation. Having power over your own emotional well-being is life-changing, and the resilience this brings allows you to completely transform your thinking and your life.

## THE FOUNDATION OF FORGIVENESS

You have now built a foundation upon which other growth can occur. It wouldn't be wise to build a house without a solid foundation, nor is it a good idea to build a life without a solid foundation built on the values of forgiveness, resilience, and emotional well-being. With this type of foundation in your life, you can weather any storm because you know where your values lie and how to meet life's challenges without losing your balance.

I encourage you to apply the principles in this book to all areas of your life as you move forward in healing and forgiveness. They will work with any challenge because they are life principles.

# CONCLUSION

Forgiveness is an accessible superpower everyone can harness, capable of transforming pain and hardship into strength, peace, and a renewed sense of purpose. The journey to the freedom of forgiveness isn't easy, but it is necessary if you want to be free from anger and resentment.

To recap, here are some of the key points we've covered throughout this book:

### 1. Acknowledge Your Pain

1. Before dealing with the anger and resentment, you must acknowledge the pain that caused it.
2. You need to allow yourself to go through the stages of forgiveness (much like grief), which are:

   a. Acknowledgment
   b. Understanding
   c. Empathy

    d. Decision
    e. Release

## 2. Debunking Some of the Myths Around Forgiveness

1. You have a choice not to be a victim.
2. Forgiveness isn't a weakness.
3. You don't have to reconcile with the person who wronged you.
4. Forgiveness doesn't mean condoning the wrong actions of the other person.
5. Forgiveness isn't forgetting.

## 3. Navigating the Difference Between Forgiveness and Reconciliation

1. Reconciliation isn't necessary for forgiveness and often isn't even recommended.
2. They are two entirely separate processes.

## 4. The Role of Empathy in Forgiving Others

1. Empathy is a huge help in releasing forgiveness to someone as it helps give you insight into the reasons behind their actions.
2. Hurt people often hurt other people; empathy helps us understand this.
3. The world is unfair; people are unfair.

### 5. Self-Forgiveness Is Vital to Healing

1. Forgiving yourself is one of the most powerful things you can do for yourself.
2. Allow yourself to be human and understand that you don't always have control or foresight over what your choices may bring to your life.

### 6. The Powerful Effect Forgiveness Has on Your Health

1. There is a link between bitterness and the development of cancer.
2. We need to think about how our emotions are affecting our bodies and how to better self-regulate.
3. Unexpressed emotions can be like toxins in your body.

### 7. Setting Boundaries and How Vital They Are to Healthy Relationships

1. This is one of the hardest things to do if your parents don't have healthy boundaries, but it's one of the best things you can learn for your mental health.
2. Setting boundaries can be the easiest part; keeping them intact around people who are determined to push them can be challenging.
3. We discussed how to set and maintain healthy boundaries and communicate them to the people in your life.

### 8. Forgiveness as a Lifestyle

1. Forgiveness isn't just a one-and-done thing; it's a lifestyle and a mindset that will aid you in all areas of your life.
2. Control is an illusion; we only have control over our actions and reactions.
3. Choose to be a survivor rather than a victim.

### 9. Identifying What Holds You Back

1. Sometimes, you start on a journey, but roadblocks hold you back from real progress.
2. Identifying what is in your way can help you deal with those issues so you can continue your forgiveness journey.
3. Trust isn't a given.
4. Just because someone is a family member or in a close relationship with you doesn't mean you must trust them.
5. Being wise about who you trust or how much you trust can safeguard your heart from further pain.
6. It's vital to find balance and communicate that to the people you are relating to.

### 10. Strategies for Addressing Trauma

1. A journal can be your best friend and help you to communicate with your inner self.
2. Meditation helps calm the mind and address the issues holding you back from true freedom.

### 11. The Fear of Weakness Is a Substantial Barrier

1. You might not want to seem weak, but choosing forgiveness over anger and resentment takes strength.
2. Watch out for your ego taking over the journey.
3. Anger and bitterness are strong foes.
4. Anger is an emotion and isn't wrong, but allowing it to take over your life is like putting yourself in handcuffs and trying to drive the car of your life.
5. One of the most powerful things you can do is forgive and allow the anger and bitterness to dissolve.

### 12. How to Release Anger

1. Self-awareness
2. Mindfulness and deep breathing
3. Journaling
4. Communication
5. Exercise
6. Creative Expression
7. Gratitude
8. Boundaries
9. Seek professional help
10. Reflect and adjust

### 13. Overcoming Victim Mentality

1. You aren't a victim; you WERE a victim.
   Understanding the difference can transform your life.
2. It's about your mindset, not your experience.
3. Be a survivor, not a victim.

### 14. Can You Forgive Without an Apology?

1. Sometimes, the fear of facing another person can hold you back from forgiveness.
2. A desire for justice can stop your progress.
3. Empathy, self-reflection, and acceptance are paths to freedom and joy.

### 15. Letting Go of Control

1. You have NO CONTROL.
2. It's okay not to have control because you can control your own actions.
3. Release yourself from the need to control and release the burden of fear.

### 16. Practical Steps to Forgiveness

1. Journaling "morning pages"
2. Meditation

   a. Metta meditation
   b. Mindful breathing
   c. Visualization

     d. Body scan with release

     e. R.A.I.N. Meditation

## 17. The Art of Letting Go

1. It is a powerful choice to let go; it's not giving up but release.
2. Using rituals can be an effective way to assist in letting go.
3. Visualization is powerful.
4. Visualize the situation to help in releasing it.
5. You deserve to be free; visualize yourself in complete freedom.

## 18. Forgiveness Affirmations

1. Affirmations are a great daily reminder to pay attention to your thoughts.

## 19. Release Control to Find It

## 20. Forgiving in Layers

1. There are many layers to forgiveness.
2. You may have to repeat the process each time you peel back a layer, but it's normal.

## 21. The Healing Power of Empathy

1. Seeing the other side.
2. The difference between empathy and sympathy.

3. Empathy doesn't mean feeling sorry for the person who hurt you; it means helping you understand why they did it.
4. Perspective-taking exercises to help see the other person's perspective.
5. Active listening and how to pay attention in an effective way.
6. Storytelling and shared experiences foster a sense of mutual understanding and vulnerability.

### 22. Rebuilding Trust

1. Clear and open communication is needed for any relationship to heal and move forward.

### 23. Celebrating Small Victories

1. You may feel you're not progressing, but celebrating small victories can help you see your progress.
2. Milestones are a great way to mark progress.
3. Write in your journal or tell a friend about your progress. You can then be reminded later when you're feeling down.

### 24. What You Think About, You Bring About

1. Change your mind to change your life.

### 25. Establish Healthy Boundaries

1. Set yourself up for success by setting boundaries post-forgiveness.

2. Boundaries are an early warning system.

### 26. The Importance of Self-Care

1. Your needs differ from others, so figure out what self-care means for you.
2. Journal about your needs to receive more insight.
3. Your body will let you know if you haven't cared for yourself.

### 27. Gratitude is Vital

1. Keeping your mind on gratitude helps to keep bitterness at bay.
2. A forgiving heart leads to a peaceful life.

### 28. Navigating Relationships With Forgiveness

1. If you expect to be offended, you will be.
2. Loving someone means allowing them to be human.
3. Having boundaries in your relationship is vital.

### 29. Resilience Through Forgiveness

1. Build emotional strength with resilience and a forgiveness mindset.

### 30. Forgive and Let Go of the Past

1. Envision a future unburdened by the past.
2. If you're not growing, you're dying.
3. Forgiveness is a superpower.

## 31. Personal Stories of Transformation

If you've been on your forgiveness journey while reading the book, take some time to reflect on your journey, writing in your journal about the struggles you've faced along the way and how you overcame them. Think about the steps you've taken, whether you've forgiven the person who hurt you or written a letter and burned it—all the things you've done that are necessary for you to come to the freedom of forgiveness. This reflection will be valuable as you continue your life journey and work on other areas.

Now is the time to start if you haven't yet begun your journey. You don't want to waste any more time having pain and anger control your thoughts or your life. Each of these steps and suggestions has proven to work in many people's lives, including my own. If you struggle to know where to begin, please get in touch with professionals for help, but don't give up. Community support, such as professional therapists, counselors, and support networks, are available. Whatever your needs are, there is someone there to assist you. You can take the book and work through the chapters and steps together.

You are not alone. We have all experienced deep pain, although at different degrees and from different sources. Pain is unique to each person. That doesn't make one person more important than another. Please don't be afraid to ask for help; we can all understand how complicated this process can be. Even though it can be challenging, the rewards are so great that it's worth whatever you must endure. I have gone through it and know you can do it, too. Even if you must take a slower pace, that's okay. You can only do what you can handle. Don't beat yourself up but be empathic to yourself and to the people around you who are supporting you.

Forgiveness can be your superpower; all you need to do is choose to begin. Take it one day, one step at a time, and you will get there. I believe in you!

# REFERENCES

Adamos, M., & Griffin, J. (n.d.). *What Do We Mean by "Forgiveness?": Some answers from the ancient Greeks.* PhilArchive. https://philarchive.org/archive/ADAWDW

Associates, S. C. (2021, October 25). *The path to forgiveness in five steps.* Stonebriar Counseling Associates. https://www.stonebriarca.com/the-path-to-forgiveness-in-five-steps/

Bank Lees, A. (2018, November 13). *Forgiveness: the path to healing and emotional freedom.* Psychology Today. https://www.psychologytoday.com/ca/blog/surviving-thriving/201811/forgiveness-the-path-healing-and-emotional-freedom

*Corrie ten Boom.* (2019, November 30). Wikipedia. https://en.wikipedia.org/wiki/Corrie_ten_Boom

Enright, R. (2015, October 15). *Eight keys to forgiveness.* Greater Good. https://greatergood.berkeley.edu/article/item/eight_keys_to_forgiveness

*Forgiveness.* (2022). American Psychological Association. https://www.apa.org/topics/forgiveness#:

Gupta, S. (2023, June 20). *What does the term "emotional baggage" mean?* Verywell Mind. https://www.verywellmind.com/emotional-baggage-symptoms-causes-and-coping-strategies-6742778

James, J. (2020, August 2). *The fourfold path to forgiveness: a way to release hurt and resentment.* Medium. https://jenniferjames-author.medium.com/the-fourfold-path-to-forgiveness-a-way-to-release-hurt-and-resentment-41c290af819b

McGraw, Dr., P. (2014, January 22). *Dr. Phil: You Teach People How to Treat You. Oprah.com.* https://www.oprah.com/spirit/teach-people-how-to-treat-you-dr-phils-advice#:

Murnan, A. (2023, August 21). *Emotions trapped in the body: Symptoms and release.* Medical News Today. https://www.medicalnewstoday.com/articles/emotions-trapped-in-the-body#concept

Park, W. (2020, November 9). *What other cultures can teach us about forgiveness.* BBC. https://www.bbc.com/future/article/20201109-what-other-cultures-can-teach-us-about-forgiveness

Strauss Cohen Ph.D., E. (2023, September 11). *The importance of compassion and empathy when forgiving.* Psychology Today. https://www.psychology today.com/us/blog/your-emotional-meter/202309/the-importance-of-compassion-and-empathy-when-forgiving

Thomas, S. P., Groer, M., Davis, M., Droppleman, P., Mozingo, J., & Pierce, M. (2000). Anger and cancer. *Cancer Nursing, 23*(5), 344–349. https://doi.org/10.1097/00002820-200010000-00003

Vanbuskirk, S. (2021, August 19). *The mental health effects of holding a grudge.* Verywell Mind. https://www.verywellmind.com/the-mental-health-effects-of-holding-a-grudge-5176186

Weir, K. (2017). *Forgiveness can improve mental and physical health.* American Psychological Association. https://www.apa.org/monitor/2017/01/ce-corner

Zugaro, M. (2021, August 2). *To forgive others, you first have to forgive yourself.* Mind Cafe. https://medium.com/mind-cafe/to-forgive-others-you-first-have-to-forgive-yourself-fb00751b8171

Made in the USA
Las Vegas, NV
24 October 2024

10415836R00080